DENALI NATIONAL PARK

DON PITCHER

Contents

DENALI NATIONAL PARK AND VICINITY

Spectacular Denali National Park is near the center of Alaska, 235 miles north of Anchorage and 125 miles south of Fairbanks. The park covers nearly six million acres of land on both sides of the Alaska Range, and is part of the vast Interior Alaska terrain of boreal forests, tundra, and towering mountains.

The Parks Highway connecting Anchorage with Denali and Fairbanks is the only paved route through this country. Other roads are more limited: a dirt road extends 90 miles through Denali National Park, and the gravel Denali Highway turns east from Cantwell paralleling the Alaska Range to Paxson, but the rest of the land has few roads.

One of the wonderful aspects of Alaska's Interior is its vastness. Although Talkeetna and the entrance to Denali National Park are both packed with travelers all summer long, it's amazingly easy to escape the crowds and find yourself in a land that seems unchanged from time immemorial. Take the time to pull off the highway and fish a bit on one of the creeks or climb a hill for the view. You won't regret it!

PLANNING YOUR TIME

It's a very scenic five-hour drive (eight relaxing hours by train) from Anchorage to the entrance to **Denali National Park.** The big draws are 20,320-foot Mount McKinley (often obscured by clouds), a grand landscape of open tundra and boreal forests, and

HIGHLIGHTS

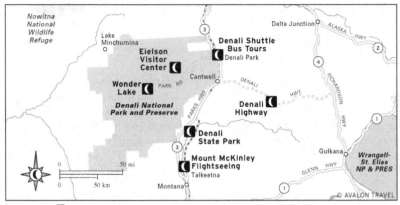

LOOK FOR ◖ TO FIND RECOMMENDED SIGHTS, ACTIVITIES, DINING, AND LODGING.

◖ **Mount McKinley Flightseeing:** Talkeetna is the base for several air charter operators with flights over McKinley that include a bush plane landing on Ruth Glacier (page 9).

◖ **Denali State Park:** This 325,000-acre park affords breathtaking views of Mount McKinley from backcountry trails and roadside pullouts (page 21).

◖ **Denali Highway:** This 136-mile mostly gravel road provides dramatic views of the Alaska Range and access to vast stretches of wild country (page 23).

◖ **Denali Shuttle Bus Tours:** This is the only way to reach the heart of Alaska's most famous park. Grizzlies, moose, wolves, and Dall sheep are commonly seen and you may even see Mount McKinley in all its glory (page 34).

◖ **Eielson Visitor Center:** A four-hour one-way ride by shuttle bus, this modern eco-friendly visitor center provides spectacular views of Denali when the mountain is out (page 38).

◖ **Wonder Lake:** Near the end of the Park Road, Wonder Lake is famous for picture-perfect views of the mountain (page 38).

the chance to watch grizzly bears, moose, wolves, Dall sheep, and caribou. Private cars are not allowed on the 92-mile Park Road, but **shuttle and tour buses** provide a wonderful way to see the park or to access remote areas for hiking and camping. Be sure to book your bus well in advance of your trip since the seats often fill up.

It's 8 hours round-trip to **Eielson Visitor Center,** where most buses turn around, or a challenging 11 hours round-trip to **Wonder Lake,** deep inside the park. Plan to take at least two days—more if at all possible—to explore

the park; one day for a ride into the park, and the second for a half-day ranger-led Discovery Hike or other trek. Add another day for a float down the Nenana River just outside the park entrance and to take in the sled dog demonstrations and other activities.

Talkeetna is a delightful destination, with outstanding vistas across to Mount McKinley and a quaint historic downtown filled with mountaineers and outdoor enthusiasts. Several air-taxi operators offer Mount McKinley flightseeing trips that often include a glacier landing. Farther north is the **Denali Highway,**

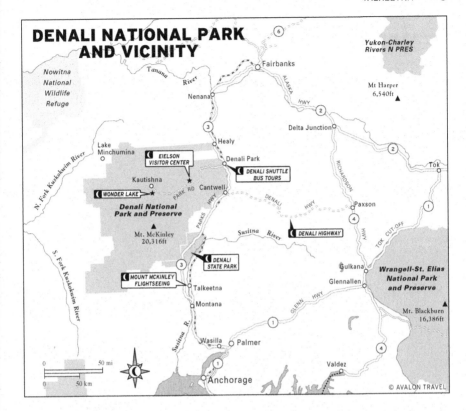

DENALI NATIONAL PARK AND VICINITY

Yukon-Charley Rivers N PRES

Nowitna National Wildlife Refuge

Tanana River

Nenana

Fairbanks

Mt Harper 6,540ft ▲

Delta Junction

Lake Minchumina

EIELSON VISITOR CENTER

Healy

Denali Park

DENALI SHUTTLE BUS TOURS

Tok

Kautishna

WONDER LAKE

Cantwell

PARK RD

Denali National Park and Preserve

Paxson

DENALI HIGHWAY

Mt. McKinley 20,316ft ▲

Susitna River

PARKS HWY

N. Fork Kuskokwim River

S. Fork Kuskokwim River

DENALI STATE PARK

MOUNT MCKINLEY FLIGHTSEEING

Talkeetna

Montana

Gulkana

Glennallen

Wrangell-St. Elias National Park and Preserve

Mt. Blackburn 16,386ft ▲

Susitna R.

Wasilla

Palmer

GLENN HWY

Anchorage

Valdez

0   50 mi
0   50 km

© AVALON TRAVEL

a partly paved, mostly gravel 126-mile route that cuts east to west along the magnificent Alaska Range. One could easily spend several days hiking backcountry routes, camping beneath the midnight sun, and fishing the lakes and streams along the Denali Highway.

Talkeetna

The outdoorsy and youthful town of Talkeetna (pop. 900) lies at the end of a 14-mile side road that splits away from the Parks Highway 98 miles north of Anchorage. Two closely related phenomena dominate this small bush community: The Mountain, and flying to and climbing on The Mountain. On a clear day, from the overlook a mile out on the Spur Road, Mount McKinley and the accompanying Alaska Range scrape the sky like a jagged white wall.

All summer, local flightseeing and air-taxi companies take off in a continuous parade to circle Mount McKinley, buzz up long glaciers or even land on them, then return to Talkeetna's busy airport to drop off passengers whose wide eyes, broad smiles, and shaky knees attest to the excitement of this once-in-a-lifetime thrill. In late April-early July, these same special "wheel-and-ski" planes might be delivering an American, European, Japanese,

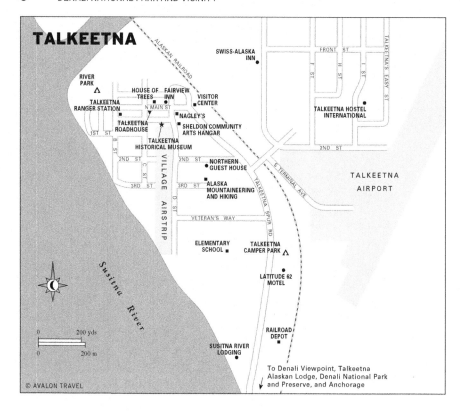

or Korean climbing expedition to the Kahiltna Glacier (elev. 7,000 ft.), from which—if they're lucky—they inch their way up the popular West Buttress route 13,000 feet to the peak. On a clear day, if you're anywhere within striking distance, make a beeline for Talkeetna and be whisked away to some of the most stunning and alien scenery you'll ever see.

If you visit Talkeetna early in the summer you'll find a peculiar mixing of people: the earthy locals with their beards and rusty pickups, the mountaineers—mostly male—decked in color-coordinated Gore-Tex, and the busloads of cruise ship passengers who unload on the south side of town and wander through town.

Talkeetna ("where the rivers meet"), nesting at the confluence of the Talkeetna, Chulitna,

and Susitna Rivers, was originally settled by trappers and prospectors who paddled up the Susitna River to gain access to rich silver, coal, and fur country around the Talkeetna Mountains. The settlement got a boost when the railroad was pushed through in the early 1920s, and it still remains a popular stop on the route. In 1965 the Spur Road from the Parks Highway to Talkeetna was completed, providing further access to the town.

This is one of the few Alaskan villages that still looks the way people imagine Alaskan towns should look, with rustic log buildings lining Main Street and a local population that embraces both grizzled miners and back-to-the-earth tree huggers. Talkeetna men easily win the prize for the highest number of beards

DON PITCHER

Talkeetna welcome sign

per capita anywhere in Alaska! Local bumper stickers proclaim "Talkeetna, where the road ends and life begins." If you ever saw *Northern Exposure* on TV, this is the place it's rumored to have been modeled on.

SIGHTS

At mile 13 of the Talkeetna Spur Road (one mile south of town), a turnout provides a good view of **Mount McKinley and the Alaska Range.** Across the road is the driveway for Talkeetna Alaskan Lodge, where the spacious back deck provides even more striking vistas of The Mountain.

Talkeetna is a walk-around town, with most of the action within a couple of blocks of Nagley's Store and the Fairview Inn. Start your tour of town at **Nagley's Store** (13650 E. Main St., 907/733-3663, www.nagleysstore. com), a red log building that first opened in the 1920s and moved to the present site in 1945. The crowded interior has limited groceries,

espresso, and a genuine old-time atmosphere. Head up the stairs for outdoor supplies and to check out the noisy parakeets and zebra finches. The walls are lined with old photos, furs, traps, and snowshoes, and you can use the computer to check email. Look around for **Stubbs,** Talkeetna's unofficial mayor asleep in his cat box. Stubbs periodically wanders through town, frequenting West Rib Deli and Pub, directly behind Nagley's. You might be sitting at the bar in the evening when suddenly a cat jumps up to drink from his specially labeled wine glass filled with catnip-laced water. Only in Talkeetna!

The town's other icon—**Fairview Inn** (101 Main St., 907/733-2423, www.denali-fairview. com)—sits kitty-corner across the road. Locals sit on the benches out front most afternoons, and music spills out when evening comes. Built in 1923, it's a great place to soak up the old-time atmosphere, and it's entirely smoke-free. But it *is* a bar, so kids don't belong. President Warren Harding ate lunch at the Fairview during his Alaska visit in 1923; it was one of the last meals he had before falling ill and dying.

For a graphic and detailed look at the history of the town and its connection to The Mountain, check out the excellent **Talkeetna Historical Museum** (907/733-2487, www.talkeetnahistoricalsociety.org, daily 10am-6pm mid-May-Sept., by appointment the rest of the year, $3 adults, children under 12 free). Take a left after Nagley's Store; the museum is a half-block down the side street on the right in a red schoolhouse built in 1936. Inside are all sorts of local artifacts—including a horsehide coat from the 1890s—but more interesting is the old railroad section house out back, which now houses an enormous relief map of Denali surrounded by photos and the stories of climbers, including several famous adventurers who lost their lives on this treacherous peak. Other exhibits show the gear climbers use, such as the required "clean mountain cans" for

© DON PITCHER

Nagley's Store

transporting human waste. Return at 1pm for a Park Service ranger talk on climbing Mount McKinley.

ENTERTAINMENT AND EVENTS

Fairview Inn (101 Main St., 907/733-2423, www.denali-fairview.com) has live bands five nights a week in the summer, and on winter Saturdays.

The **Sheldon Community Arts Hangar** (downtown behind Nagley's, 907/733-2321 or 800/478-2321, June-Aug., showtimes daily 3 and 7pm) hosts plays and other events in the summer, including showings of a video on the life of legendary bush pilot Don Sheldon, who used this building as his airplane hangar.

Talkeetna loves to party, especially on the **Fourth of July** with a parade and other events. All summer long you can find music in the downtown park during **Live at 5** (Fri.) performances.

Winter arrives with a vengeance this far

north, and **Talkeetna Winterfest** (Dec.) brightens spirits, especially those of the many local bachelors. The main events are a Wilderness Woman Contest that includes all sorts of wacky activities, followed later that evening by a Bachelor Society Ball during which local bachelors are bid on by single women, many of whom drive up from Anchorage for the chance. It has all the sexual energy of a male-stripper night, except that some of the men are considerably less fit and keep their clothes on (at least during the bidding). This is one of Alaska's most authentic winter events, representing the skewed ratio of men to women and the oddball nature of small-town Alaska.

SHOPPING

Talkeetna's **Artisans Open Air Market** (no phone, Sat.-Mon. 10am-6pm summer) has booths selling jewelry, clothing, and local crafts. It's in front of the Sheldon Community Arts Hangar behind Nagley's.

The Dancing Leaf Gallery (Main St. near Nagley's, 907/733-5323, www.thedancingleafgallery.com) has a fine selection of local and Alaskan art in a lovely timber frame building.

Several local shops are worth a visit, including the downtown **Denali Images Art Gallery** (22336 S. Talkeetna Spur, 907/733-2026), which displays wildlife and nature images from a half-dozen local photographers.

Find paintings by David Totten at **Wildlife North Art Gallery** (Mile 10 Talkeetna Spur Rd., 907/733-5811, www.davidtotten.com).

Kahiltna Birchworks (Mile 1 Talkeetna Spur Rd., 907/733-1409 or 800/380-7457, www.alaskawildharvest.com, daily mid-May-mid-Sept.) is a unique local business where owners Michael and Dulce East produce distinctively tart-sweet birch syrup and other products. They tap more than 10,000 birch trees each spring, using a sophisticated maze of tubing to produce 140,000 gallons of sap and 1,300 gallons of golden syrup. This is the

© DON PITCHER

Talkeetna Historical Museum

world's largest producer of birch syrup; okay, there isn't a lot of competition out there. Taste a sample or buy a bottle of syrup at their facility, check out the Alaskan-made gifts, or get scoops of birch flavored Matanuska Creamery ice cream topped with berry toppings. Have a picnic on the porch. Visit in early May to watch them in full production mode.

RECREATION
◖ Mount McKinley Flightseeing

Talkeetna is famous as a launching point for flights over Mount McKinley, and on a clear summer day a constant parade of planes takes off from the airport on the edge of town. The flight services in town offer a bewildering array of possibilities, including short scenic flights, glacier landings, drop-off hiking or fishing, wildlife-viewing, overnight trips, and flights to, around, or over the top of The Mountain. Rates vary according to the type of airplane, length of the flight, and how many

people there are in your group. Most outfits will try to match you up with other folks to maximize your flightseeing dollar. Be flexible in your plans, since weather is infinitely variable and is always the most important consideration when it comes to flying you safely. There are one-hour flights ($200 pp, $275 pp with a glacier landing), but the most popular tours are 1.25 hours long ($250-265 pp, $325-340 pp with a glacier landing). A 1.5-hour flight ($385 pp with a glacier landing) to the summit of Mount McKinley offers a good chance to see the climbers. Given the choice, I'd always pay a bit more for the glacier landing on any of these. It turns a spectacular flight into a once-in-a-lifetime adventure.

Reservations are recommended, but not always necessary, so stop by the airport for details and current weather conditions around The Mountain. Note that the climbing season on Mount McKinley runs from early spring until mid- or late June, and the flight services

Talkeetna is the primary starting point for Denali flightseeing trips.

are busiest then. As always with bush flying, risks are involved, and fatalities have taken the lives of some of the best local pilots and climbers over the years. Your odds (not to mention the vistas) are probably better if you wait until a clear day to fly.

A number of charter companies provide service to Mount McKinley from the Talkeetna Airport. **K2 Aviation** (907/733-2291 or 800/764-2291, www.flyk2.com) and **Talkeetna Air Taxi** (907/733-2218 or 800/533-2219, www.talkeetnaair.com) are the largest operators. Talkeetna Air is a favorite of climbers, and provides translations for Korean and Japanese travelers. K2 provides printed material translated in multiple languages to help identify features during the flight. K2 offers a unique fly-in trip that includes a floatplane trip to remote Moraine Lake where you hike into the backcountry. These four-hour trips ($495 pp) are only offered after ice melts from the lake in mid-June.

Owned by Holly Sheldon—daughter of famed pilot Don Sheldon—**Sheldon Air Service** (907/733-2321 or 800/478-2321, www.

sheldonairservice.com) is an excellent small family operation offering a personal touch.

Based at Fish Lake, **Alaska Bush Floatplane Service** (Mile 9 Talkeetna Spur Rd., 907/733-1693 or 877/710-8807, www.alaskafloatplane.com) offers flightseeing into Denali, but is better known for fly-in hiking, bear-viewing, and fishing at remote lakes.

Talkeetna Aero Services (907/683-2899 or 888/733-2899, www.talkeetnaaero.com) has flightseeing from Talkeetna (no glacier landings from here), with a larger operation out of Healy that goes by the name of Denali Air.

River Trips

Denali View Raft Adventures (907/733-2778 or 877/533-2778, www.denaliviewraft.com) has 3-hour Susitna River trips ($105 adults, $65 children), 2-hour Talkeetna River floats ($75 adults, $49 children), and a unique 4.5-hour trip that starts with a train ride upriver followed by a float and lunch on the Susitna River ($169 adults, $110 children).

Talkeetna River Guides (907/733-2677 or

800/353-2677, www.talkeetnariverguides.com) offers two-hour Talkeetna River natural history floats ($79 adults, $59 children) and four-hour Chulitna River trips ($129 adults, $109 children). They primarily book customers from the large hotels. **Mahay's Riverboat Service** (907/733-2223 or 800/736-2210, www.mahaysriverboat.com) has a popular two-hour jet-boat tour up the Susitna River ($65 adults, $49 children). Longer trips are also offered, including a five-hour run into Devil's Canyon ($155 adults, $116 children).

The fishing in Talkeetna is excellent all summer long; rainbow trout, grayling, Dolly Varden, and all five species of Pacific salmon are there for the catching. Local riverboat services can supply you with a fishing guide or drop you off along the river for the day or overnight. The visitor center has rack cards from most local guides, including **Phantom Salmon Charters** (907/733-2322, www.phantomsalmoncharters.com).

Ziplining

Talkeetna's newest adventure is **Denali Zipline Tours** (13572 E. Main St., 907/733-3988 or 855/733-3988, www.denaliziplinetours.com, $149 adults, $119 ages 10-14, no children under 10 allowed), located in a birch, spruce, and cottonwood forest three miles from town. The course consists of nine ziplines and three skybridges, with panoramic views of Denali and the Alaska Range along the way. The highest platform is 60 feet up a tree, and the final zipline—700 feet long—takes you over a small lake. Tours take place several times a day all summer, with a maximum of eight guests for two guides. This is a good rainy day alternative when flights to McKinley are cancelled.

Biking, Hiking, and Canoeing

A paved bike path parallels the Spur Road all the way to Talkeetna. Turn off onto gravel roads at Miles 3 and 12 for out-of-the-way lakes and camping spots. At Mile 13 is the big turnout with an interpretive sign on the Alaska Range and heart-stopping views if the clouds are cooperating. Talkeetna Alaskan Lodge is on the opposite side of the road; stop in for the Mount McKinley view from its back deck even if you aren't overnighting here.

It's hard to miss the florescent green bikes from **Talkeetna Bike Rentals** (22911 S. Talkeetna Spur Rd., 907/354-1222, www.talkeetnabikerentals.com, $20 for three hours), located at the big parking lot just before you enter town. These are primarily for the cruise ship crowd, with three-speeds, cruisers, and trikes, along with tag alongs and baby bugs. They're a bit spendy for a three-hour rental of a cruiser bike.

Two miles south of town, **Talkeetna Lakes Park** (off Comsat Rd., www.matsugov.us) covers more than a thousand acres of forested land around X, Y, and Z Lakes. There is no camping, but the parks have a maze of excellent hiking and biking trails that become cross-country ski trails in winter. Several canoes are stashed at the park; rent one from **Talkeetna Camp and Canoe** (907/733-3355 or 800/318-2534, www.talkeetnacampandcanoe.com, canoes $35/day).

Alaska Nature Guides (907/733-1237, www.alaskanatureguides.com, mid-May-mid-Sept., $59 adults, $39 children) provides excellent three-hour nature walks within Talkeetna Lakes Park. The guides are former national park rangers with years of local experience, and also offer custom birding, photography, and winter snowshoeing trips.

If your kids are bored, take them to the big **Talkeetna Playground** on the south end of town.

Horseback Riding and Dog Mushing

Join a ride through the birch forests through **Talkeetna Horses** (3.1 miles up Montana Creek Rd., off Parks Hwy. Mile 96.1,

907/733-0154, www.talkeetnahorses.com, daily May-mid-Sept., $50 one-hour ride, $65 half-day ride, $100 dinner ride). Dinner rides consist of one hour on horseback plus a steak dinner around a campfire.

Tour the kennels of Iditarod musher Jerry Sousa and take a cart ride behind a team of sled dogs at **Sundog Racing Kennel** (Main St., 907/733-3355 or 800/318-2534, www.sundog-kennel.com, $75 pp two-hour tour, $150 10-mile trip). There are two-hour kennel tours and rides, or for the real deal, join a 10-mile winter-time dog mushing trip.

Another Iditarod competitor, Randy Cummins of **Huskytown Kennel** (30018 Talkeetna Spur Rd., 907/733-4759, www.hus-kytown.com, $35 pp), has similar tours.

ACCOMMODATIONS

There is a 5 percent lodging tax in Talkeetna; add the tax to the base price of your lodging choice.

Hostels

Right in the center of Main Street, **House of 7 Trees** (Main St., 907/733-7733, late Apr.-early Sept., hostel bunks $25 pp, guest rooms $75-90) is a lovely and clean little place that attracts travelers of all ages and nationalities. Built in 1936, this charming frame home has lots of history, and the friendly owner Pat McGee—a 35-year Talkeetna resident—really knows the area. Her welcoming dog adds to the allure. The back cabin houses six coed hostel bunks, and four private rooms are upstairs in the main house. Three of the private rooms have one queen or two twin beds, and the fourth private room contains a queen and twin bed—all topped with hand-made quilts. Guests can access the common room with its baby grand piano, plus the impressive commercial kitchen, two baths (one wheelchair accessible), and the shady yard. Wi-Fi is available. Make reservations a few weeks ahead, especially for summer weekends, but don't call after 9:30pm. There is no alcohol here.

A few blocks east of downtown near the airport, **Talkeetna Hostel International** (22159 S. I St., 907/733-4678, www.talkeetnahostel. com, mid-Apr.-Sept., dorm rooms $22 pp; guest rooms $50-65 d; cabin $50, add $10 pp for extra guests; VW bus $25 s, $35 d; tents $10) is a place with haphazard management that may or may not be to your taste. The location is quiet and shady. Each of the two coed dorm rooms has four beds. There are also private rooms and a very basic cabin with two twin beds and a miniscule loft. Another option (though not recommended) is the ancient VW bus. You can also pitch a tent in the backyard. There are three baths, a kitchen and laundry, guest computer, Wi-Fi, TV, and no curfew.

Hotels

For a taste of the past, stay at **Talkeetna Roadhouse** (corner of Main St. and C St., 907/733-1351, www.talkeetnaroadhouse.com, hostel $20 pp; guest rooms $55-75 s, $65-85 d shared bath; cabin $105 for two, add $10 pp for extra guests, maximum of five), a delightful old Alaskan lodge, constructed in 1917 and in business since 1944. It's best known for home-cooked meals downstairs, but it also has lodging options. Budget travelers and mountaineers appreciate the Roadhouse's four-bed coed hostel with a bath down the hall. Five simple but clean guest rooms have period antiques and shared baths. Out back is a cozy little cabin that sleeps two. It has a fridge, microwave, TV, and gas fireplace, with bathrooms in the main building. Three blocks away is Trapper John's cabin ($130 d), with two double beds, fridge, microwave, running water, and a private bath. Also available is an apartment ($150 d private bath), located over the historic red schoolhouse at the museum.

Latitude 62 Motel (next to the airport and railroad depot, 907/733-2262, www.lati-tude62.com, $85 d, suite $120 d, offsite cabin $130 d) is a two-story log building on the south end of town with 11 small budget rooms and a suite. The furnishings are older, and there are no phones or TVs, but Latitude does have Wi-Fi, plus a full service restaurant and bar. An offsite log cabin includes a private bath with jetted tub and full kitchen.

Downtown above Wildflower Café, **Main St. Suites** (Main St., 907/733-2694, www.talkeetnasuites.com, summer only, studio $150 d, suite $175 d) consists of a one-bedroom studio and a two-bedroom suite, both with private baths and kitchenettes.

Head across the railroad tracks to **Swiss-Alaska Inn** (22056 S. F St., 907/733-2424, www.swissalaska.com, $108 s, $135-150 d, cabin $165), with 20 motel rooms, homemade quilts, and private baths. There is also a separate cabin with three beds, a kitchenette, and private bath. There is no TV reception, but videos are available along with Wi-Fi. German is spoken, and the adjacent restaurant (open seasonally) serves good breakfasts.

Talkeetna Alaskan Lodge (23601 Talkeetna Spur Rd., 907/733-9500 or 888/959-9590, www.talkeetnalodge.com, mid-May-mid-Sept., $279-315 d, $409 d for rooms that face Mount McKinley; suites $479-569 d) sits atop a hill a mile south of Talkeetna, with spacious, modern rooms. There are also luxury suites, most with gas fireplaces and jetted tubs. The grand lobby includes a stone fireplace and towering windows framing The Mountain, and a fine-dining restaurant is on the premises. There's a free shuttle to town and the train depot. This 200-room Native Alaskan-owned lodge serves up million-dollar views for an upscale clientele, pretty much the opposite of most Talkeetna lodging places. The hotel is packed with cruise ship passengers all summer.

Cabins

Paradise Lodge & Cabins (S. Birch Creek Blvd., 907/733-1471 or 888/205-3553, www.paradiselodge.net, mid-May-early Sept., $115

© DON PITCHER

Talkeetna Alaskan Lodge

d, add $10 pp for extra guests) is aptly named, with a peaceful and secluded location along Fish Lake five miles south of Talkeetna. Four rustic log cabins (with double beds and kitchenettes but no running water) share a bathhouse, or you can stay in the main lodge where two rooms share a bath. Also available is a spacious three-bedroom, four-bath home ($500 for up to eight guests). Wi-Fi is available, but TVs are only in the main lodge. This off-the-grid place (power comes from a generator) is open only in the summer months.

Right in town behind Mountain High Pizza, **Talkeetna Cabins** (22137 C St., 907/733-2227 or 888/733-9933, www.talkeetnacabins.org, cabins $175 d, add $20 pp for extra guests; house $350 for 4 people, add $20 pp for max of 12) consists of four duplex log cabins and a large three-bedroom house, all with new beds, full kitchens, dishes, private baths, laundry, grill, and Wi-Fi.

Susitna River Lodging (23094 S. Talkeetna Rd., 907/733-1505 or 866/733-1505, www.susitna-river-lodging.com, cabins $249 d, lodge rooms $169-189 d, add $15 pp for extra guests) has four lovely cedar cabins and lodge rooms a half-mile south of Talkeetna. All guest rooms and cabins include private baths, kitchenettes, electric fireplaces, BBQ grills, continental breakfast, and Wi-Fi, but no TVs. They're right along the river, and the main lodge has a big porch facing the water.

Looking for a unique wilderness experience? ◖Caribou Lodge (907/733-2163, www.cariboulodgealaska.com, Mar.-Nov., $325 pp/day) has a striking location on an unnamed alpine lake near the southeast edge of Denali National Park. It's a 15-minute flight from Talkeetna ($185 pp round-trip), but a world away. Residents for more than 20 years, owners Mike and Pam Nichols provide three simple, but nicely set up cabins for guests. Lodging, meals, canoeing, and guided day hikes—abundant wildlife—are included in the rate. There's a

two-night minimum stay, and multi-night packages are available. Winter guests come for snowshoeing, cross-country skiing, and dramatic northern lights above the summit of Mount McKinley. This is a wonderful introduction to a place where TVs, phones, and the hi-tech world don't intrude. There is no indoor plumbing here!

In a quiet location, **Question Lake Cabin** (Mile 7 Talkeetna Spur Rd., 907/243-7661, www.talkeetnaquestionlakecabin.com, $95 d) sits on the north shore of this lake where you'll hear loons calling many evenings. The rustic cabin is large enough for families, with two beds and a queen futon, plus a kitchenette. The bedside commode and outhouse remind you that this isn't the city.

Talkeetna Lakeside Cabins (35320 S. St. John Dr., 907/733-2349, www.talkeetnalakesidecabins.com, $110-150 d, add $20 pp for extra guests) consists of three immaculate cabins along a private lake a mile off Talkeetna Spur Road. Each has a kitchenette, private bath, and Wi-Fi. There are no TVs, but you can make your own entertainment by rowing around the artificially-constructed lake.

Guesthouses

On a hill facing the Alaska Range away from the noises of town, **Out of the Wild** (22198 S. Freedom Dr., 907/733-2701, www.talkeetnapro.com, $140 d, add $15 pp for extra guests) has a cluster of three architecturally unique guesthouses. Co-owner Brian McCullough (an internationally known mountaineer and guide) built them all by hand, filling each with distinctive furnishings. All three places contain private baths and full kitchens stocked with breakfast supplies, Wi-Fi, and satellite TVs. Spacious Mountain House has three upstairs bedrooms and two baths, Kahiltna Chalet is an elegant cottage perfect for romantic getaways, and Stone Hut features artistic stonework, two bedrooms, and a spiral staircase. Rates are the same for all rooms at Out of the Wild. Kids and dogs are welcome, and rooms are available year-round. The hilltop location is perfect for winter northern lights viewing.

Just two blocks from Main Street, **Northern Guest House** (13712 2nd St., 907/715-4868, www.northernguesthouse.com, $60 s, $80 d, add $20 pp for extra guests) has hard to beat rates. The three guest rooms each contain a private bath and two beds, and guests can use the full kitchen, dining room, and living room, plus the rec room with a ping pong table and piano. A two-bedroom apartment ($95-115 d) contains a kitchen, living room, bath, private deck, and private entrance. Borrow a bike to explore town, or kick back around the enclosed backyard fire pit. There is no Wi-Fi here, however.

Bed-and-Breakfasts

When it comes to Talkeetna B&Bs the old "location, location, location" saying applies, with several places providing Denali vistas to die for.

Five miles from Talkeetna, **Denali Overlook Inn** (29198 S. Talkeetna Spur Rd., 907/733-3555 or 855/733-3555, www.denalioverlookinn.com, open all year, $179-279 d) is a memorable home where the view exceeds your expectations; on a clear day it's impossible to miss Mount McKinley and the rest of the Alaska Range. Five bedrooms—the largest features wall-to-wall windows facing The Mountain—have private baths, and a full menu breakfast is included, along with a guest computer and Wi-Fi. Honeymooners will appreciate privacy at the adjacent two-level cabin ($259 d) with a kitchenette and private bath.

Five miles east of town, **Traleika Mountaintop Cabins** (22216 S. Freedom Dr., 907/733-2711, www.traleika.com, guesthouse $205 d, cabins $175-185 d, add $20 pp for extra guests) has a dramatic location facing Denali. There is a two-bedroom guesthouse and two smaller cabins. All three places include full baths, living rooms, decks, kitchens, and Wi-Fi; the largest sleeps up to eight.

Not far away—with an equally fine vista—is the reasonably priced **Freedom Hills B&B** (Freedom Dr., 907/733-2455 or 888/703-2455, www.gbfreedomhillsbb.com, May-Sept., $130 d shared bath, $150 d private bath), where five guest rooms are in two adjacent homes. There's an enormous deck on the main house for Denali views, and free Wi-Fi. Co-owner and chef Bill Germain creates a delicious breakfast each morning.

Built in 1946 and beautifully maintained, **Fireweed Station Inn** (15113 E. Sunshine Rd., 907/733-1457 or 888/647-1457, www.fireweedstation.com, guest rooms $150 d, suite $205 d, cabin $100 d) is a gorgeous log home off Mile 2 of the Talkeetna Spur Road. A spacious suite occupies the entire upstairs, and downstairs are two guest rooms with private baths. A historic cabin makes a good add-on for larger groups with friends or family in the main lodge. (Cabin guests use a bath in the main building.) All rates include a full breakfast, Wi-Fi, and access to the big deck. Dinners are available upon request. Winter guests can ride the flag-stop train from Anchorage directly to Fireweed Station.

Another wonderful hilltop place with stunning Alaska Range views is **Talkeetna Chalet B&B** (Mile 10.7 Talkeetna Spur Rd., 907/733-4734, www.talkeetnachalet.net, guest rooms $139-189 d, cabins $179 d, add $20 pp for extra guests), three miles from town. Three guest rooms have private baths, and two newly built cabins contain kitchenettes and private baths. Guests can use the first two floors of the home, and amenities include big hot breakfasts, a great room with a large screen TV, Wi-Fi, guest computer, and a large seasonal hot tub on the wraparound deck.

Camping

Find camping at shady **River Park** (end of Main St., no phone, free), but it lacks running water. Also on the river, but a bit farther from town, is

Talkeetna Alaska RV (22763 S. Talkeetna Spur Rd., 907/733-2604, May-Sept., tents and RVs $20, showers $6) with in-the-trees tent and RV sites. There are no hookups, but some sites are right along the Talkeetna River. **Talkeetna Camper Park** (22763 S. Talkeetna Spur, 907/733-2693, www.talkeetnacamper.com, Apr.-Oct., RVs $32-38) has 35 wooded RV sites, plus showers and laundry; it's on the right just before you enter town.

FOOD

Talkeetna has turned into quite the spot for great inexpensive food, making it a rarity on the Alaska road system. Most places are downtown, so you can just walk a block or so to see what appeals to you.

Cafés and Diners

At ◖ **Talkeetna Roadhouse** (corner of Main St. and C St., 907/733-1351, www.talkeetnaroadhouse.com, daily 6am-9pm mid-May-mid-Sept., daily 8am-8pm winter, $5-14) long tables make for fun family-style dining with crowds of locals. The chalkboard menu lists two options: "Breakfast" and "Not Breakfast." Breakfast variations—available till 2pm—include Paul Bunyan-size cinnamon rolls, chocolate potato cake, and gargantuan sourdough hotcakes, from a starter that's been in use since 1902! The Not Breakfast options feature reindeer chili, squarebun BBQ pulled pork sandwiches, quiche, lasagna, homemade pasties, mac and cheese, sandwiches, salads, and daily soups. Fresh loaves of bread adorn the bakery cases in the afternoon.

◖ **Flying Squirrel** (Mile 11 Talkeetna Spur Rd., 907/733-6887, www.flyingsquirrelcafe.com, Tues.-Wed. 7:30am-7pm, Thurs.-Sat. 7:30am-9pm, Sun. 8am-6pm late May-late Oct.; closed Mon. year-round plus Tues. in winter, most items under $8, pizzas $10-17) hides in a birch forest four miles from town. Owner Anita Colton's bakery café is definitely worth the drive! Get a big mug of organic espresso while perusing the cases to see what looks interesting. Daily specials include quiche, soups, hot sandwiches, wraps, desserts, and breads. Pizzas emerge from the brick oven Thursday-Saturday nights in summer (Fri.-Sat. in winter), and the café has free Wi-Fi and gluten-free options.

For an in-town buzz, visit picture-perfect **Coffee a la Mer** (behind the Fairview Inn, 907/315-2891). Built in 1933, the snug cabin has a flower-filled yard and a selection of homemade scones, cookies, bagels, and more.

Quick Bites

A little trailer behind the Fairview Inn, **Payo's Thai Kitchen** (22160 S. Railroad Ave., 907/733-5503, daily 11am-9pm May-Sept., $8-14) serves curries, stir fries, soups, and other Thai favorites, including gang phanang curry, tom yum gai, and shrimp with ginger. A few tables are available outside and beneath the deck.

Looking for a late-night snack? **My Little Dumpling** (next to Wildflower Café, 907/733-3867, daily till 2am in summer, dumplings $10-14) has bowls of pelmeni dumplings, plus smoothies, spring rolls, and a big choice of black, green, and herbal teas. It's a tiny walkup place with a couple of covered picnic tables.

Brewpubs

Twister Creek Restaurant (13605 E. Main St., 907/733-2537, www.denalibrewingcompany.com, daily 11am-10pm mid-May-mid-Sept.; Mon.-Wed. 1pm-9pm, Thurs.-Sun. noon-9pm winter, $13-32) has a big front deck in the heart of town, plus a combined lunch/dinner menu ranging from fish and chips and handmade veggie burgers to prime rib and Thai coconut shrimp curry. There's a good selection of appetizers (try smoked provolone wedges), and the adjacent brewery serves 5-10 of their beers, including Single Engine Red, an Irish red ale. There is free Wi-Fi here, too.

West Rib Deli and Pub (directly behind

Nagley's Store, 907/733-3663, www.westribpub. info, daily 11:30am-11pm, $7-15) attracts climbers and locals with a tasty pub-grub menu that specializes in burgers, sandwiches, salads, seafood, and nightly specials. Everyone raves about the caribou chiliburger (an Angus burger topped with caribou chili and cheese), or try the veggie mushroom burger. Looking for a real artery clogger? The McKinley Burger drops two half-pound beef patties with Swiss and American cheese, sautéed onion, lettuce, and tomato. The bar serves Alaskan brews and Guinness. There's not much space here, but there is a side deck for summer evenings, and a back room with pool and foosball tables. Looking for the best deal? Meet the locals at the Friday-night burger-and-beer (for just $7). Hang around long enough and you're likely to encounter Stubbs, the stubby-tailed Manx cat who roams through town, garnering attention and food along the way. He's unofficially known as Mayor Stubbs (check him out on Facebook), and has drinks from his own wine glass—filled with catnip-infused water—at West Rib.

Housed in a modern log building, **Wildflower Café** (Main St., 907/733-1275, www.talkeetnasuites.com, daily 11am-9pm mid-May-mid-Sept., Fri.-Sun. 9:30am-9pm Dec.-mid-May, $30-36) serves a pub menu with halibut sandwiches, burgers, soups, salads, pizzas, and fish and chips all day, plus dinner specials such as grilled sesame salmon, pork tenderloin, and grilled chicken breast alfredo. More unusual is the outdoor bar next to Wildflower where you can work your way through 43 different beers on tap! Trivia tip of the day: Wildflower's owner/chef, Jerome Longo, previously served as chef for President George W. Bush.

Pizza

Mountain High Pizza Pie (22165 S. C St., 907/733-1234, www.pizzapietalkeetna.com, daily 11am-10pm May-Sept., Tues.-Sat. noon-8pm Oct.-Apr., pizza by the slice $4, pizzas

© DON PITCHER

Mountain High Pizza Pie

$14-33), in the purple log cabin, is a busy spot for pizza by the slice, calzones, flatbreads, salads, and subs. They have all the standard 15-inch pizzas. The Mountain High version is piled with "everything but the mosquitoes." In summer, the side deck is a great spot to enjoy your pizza with a beer (there are a dozen Alaskan brews on tap); it erupts with live music six nights a week all summer.

Sweets
Adjacent to the Fairview Inn is a seasonal ice cream stand called **Wake and Shake** (Main St., $3-5) with a steam-powered ice cream machine and four daily flavors. Get a cone or shake to go.

Markets
Nagley's Store (907/733-3663, www.nagleysstore.com) opened in the 1920s and is still the main place for (limited) groceries in town, but it has also added such staples of 21st-century life as an ATM, ice cream, and lattes.

Cubby's Marketplace IGA (14 miles south of town at the junction with Parks Hwy., 907/733-5050, Mon.-Sat. 8am-8pm, Sun. 8am-10pm) is the primary grocery store for the region, with a deli, liquor store, and ATM.

INFORMATION
The **Talkeetna Visitor Information Center** (across from the Village Park, 907/733-2688 or 800/660-2688, www.talkeetnadenali.com, daily 9am-7pm mid-May-mid-Sept.) is housed in the historic Three German Bachelors' Cabin, built in 1934. It's on the right side as you come into town. Out front is the funky and much-photographed "Welcome to Beautiful Downtown Talkeetna" sign next to a wheelbarrow overflowing with flowers.

At **Talkeetna/Denali Visitor Center** (intersection of Parks Hwy. and Talkeetna Spur Rd., 907/733-2688 or 800/660-2688, www.talkeetnadenali.com, daily 9am-7pm mid-Maymid-Sept.) look for the giant bear out front.

Both visitor centers are owned by Talkeetna Aero Services, but the always-helpful staff will book flights with any local air taxi, provide current weather conditions on Denali, set up fishing expeditions or guided hikes, book rooms at hotels and B&Bs, or just supply brochures and information on the area. The **Talkeetna Chamber of Commerce** (www.talkeetnachamber.org) has a useful website, and can send out brochures.

The Park Service's log **Talkeetna Ranger Station** (B St., 907/733-2231, www.nps.gov/dena, daily 8am-6pm mid-Apr.-early Sept., Mon.-Fri. 8am-5:30pm mid-Sept.-mid-Apr.) is a pleasant place to watch a climbing video or look over the mountaineering books.

SERVICES
Keep in touch with the outside world via the Internet at the **Talkeetna Public Library** (907/733-2359, www.matsulibraries.org/talkeetna, Mon.-Sat. 11am-6pm) on the south side of town. There's also a single computer upstairs in Nagley's; ask for the password at the counter.

Go to **Sunshine Community Health Center** (Mile 4 Talkeetna Spur Rd., 907/733-2273, Mon.-Sat. 9am-5pm) if the need arises.

Take showers and wash your clothes at **Washi-Washi** (on the south end of town). Showers are also available at **Talkeetna Alaska RV** (907/733-2604, May-Sept., $6).

GETTING THERE AND AROUND
The turnoff to Talkeetna is 100 miles north of Anchorage on the George Parks Highway, and the town is another 14 miles out on Talkeetna Spur Road.

Buses
Several companies provide van transportation connecting Talkeetna with Anchorage ($65 one way), Denali ($65 one way), and Fairbanks ($95 one way). **Alaska/Yukon Trails**

© DON PITCHER

From Talkeetna, continue on to Denali via the Alaska Railroad.

(907/479-2277 or 800/770-7275, www.alaskashuttle.com, late Apr.-Sept.) has a daily run from Anchorage to Talkeetna, Denali, and Fairbanks. **Park Connection** (907/245-0200 or 800/266-8625, www.alaskacoach.com, mid-May-mid-Sept.) provides summertime service connecting Talkeetna with Seward, Whittier, Anchorage, and Denali.

The **Alaska Bus Guy** (907/720-6541, www.alaskabusguy.com) operates an environmentally friendly hydrogen-hybrid van with service from Talkeetna to Anchorage or Denali ($67 one way). It has daily service in the summer and twice-weekly winter runs.

Sunshine Transit (907/733-2273, Mon.-Fri. 7:30am-5:30pm, $3 one way) is a local not-for-profit van service that operates along the Talkeetna Spur Road, stopping at points along the way, including Flying Squirrel Café and the Talkeetna Clinic.

Trains

The **Alaska Railroad** (907/265-2494 or 800/544-0552, www.alaskarailroad.com, $70 one way) *Denali Star* runs from Anchorage to Talkeetna. The train leaves Anchorage every morning at 8:15am and arrives in Talkeetna at 11:05am before continuing north to Denali National Park and Fairbanks. A southbound train leaves Fairbanks at 12:15pm, stopping in Denali, before reaching Talkeetna at 4:40pm. This train continues south to Anchorage, arriving at 8pm.

A local flag-stop train (stops on an as-needed basis), the *Hurricane Turn* (Thurs.-Sun. in summer, $96 round-trip), runs the 50 miles from Talkeetna north to Hurricane and back. It's a great way to see the countryside with locals. Winter travelers can get on or off the flag-stop train at points south of Talkeetna as well.

North from Talkeetna

TRAPPER CREEK AND PETERSVILLE ROAD

The minuscule settlement of Trapper Creek (pop. 350) is at Mile 115 of the Parks Highway, and 16 miles north of the junction with Talkeetna Spur Road. Petersville Road splits off at Trapper Creek, providing access to the western end of Denali State Park and offering some of the finest views of Mount McKinley. **Trapper Creek Museum** (a half-mile out on Petersville Rd., 907/733-2555, www.trappercreekmuseum.com, daily 10am-4pm late May-early Sept., closed winter, donations accepted) has a collection of local historical items and local crafts in a log cabin built in 1959. The museum is on Spruce Lane Farms, which raises miniature horses.

A number of rural subdivisions and homesteads are found along Petersville Road, and this is a popular winter destination for dog mushers and hordes of snowmobilers. The road continues all the way to old mining developments in the Petersville mining camp, 30 miles in, although the last section may not be passable without a high-clearance vehicle. Petersville Road is paved for 10 miles, then gravel the next 9 miles to the site of historic Forks Roadhouse, destroyed in a 2012 fire. The owners hope to rebuild. Beyond mile 19, the road deteriorates, though it's still passable until around mile 35. The State of Alaska is gradually making improvements, but expect several miles of rocks and slow going beyond this. A high clearance vehicle and good tires are recommended, but more than a few rental cars have made the 2.5-hour trek up Petersville Road.

Accommodations

Trapper Creek Inn & General Store (Mile 115 Parks Hwy., 907/733-2302, www.trappercrkinn.com, $99-139 d, tents $10, RVs $30) has guest rooms, camping sites, groceries, free Wi-Fi, a deli, and a coin laundry with showers.

Set along two ponds, **Gate Creek Cabins** (Mile 10.5 Petersville Rd., 907/733-1393, www.gatecreekcabins.com, $150 d, add $55 for two additional people) has eight modern log cabins—the largest has four bedrooms—with kitchens, private baths, TVs, BBQ grills, and Wi-Fi. They're really more like furnished vacation homes, with all the creature comforts in a peaceful and picturesque setting. Guests can borrow a canoe or paddleboat to cruise the ponds or try a bit of trout fishing. Be sure to ask about the mid-July bear-viewing opportunities. The cabins provide an extremely popular winter base for snowmobilers.

McKinley View B&B (near Mile 114 Parks Hwy., 907/733-1758 or 352/425-2573, www.mckinleyviewlodging.com, $115 s, $135 d) is all about the view. Take a seat on the back deck for dramatic vistas of the Alaska Range and Mount McKinley (when the weather cooperates). Four guest rooms are available, with full breakfasts, private baths and entrances, gracious owners, a guest computer, and Wi-Fi.

Alaska's Northland Inn (0.8 miles out Petersville Rd., 907/733-7377, www.alaskasnorthlandinn.com, $120 d, add $30 for additional adults) has a pair of two-level apartments with private baths, full kitchens, two queen beds, continental breakfast (summer only), and Wi-Fi. Relax in the great room with a pool table and satellite TV. In winter, the owners rent snowmobiles and provide groomed cross-country ski trails.

If you want remote, check out **Cache Creek Cabins** (Petersville Rd., 907/733-5200 summer or 907/252-1940 winter, www.cachecreekcabins.com, mid-June-Sept., $55-60 d shared bath, $150 private bath), 39 rugged miles out on the Petersville Road. Six rustic little cabins share a common bathhouse, and a nicer two-story cabin sleeps eight and has a private bath. The friendly owners can provide home-cooked meals ($15 breakfast, $15-20 dinner) and gold panning in the creek ($25/day). It's a pretty setting with wonderful views of Denali on the drive in. It is, however, a long and rough ride, so call for current road conditions before heading out.

Food

Also known as Angela's Heaven, **Trapper Creek Pizza Pub** (Mile 116 Parks Hwy., 907/733-3344, Fri.-Wed. 3pm-9pm late May-early Sept., Fri.-Mon. 1pm-8pm winter, $15-29) is well worth a stop. Pizza is the primary draw, but owner Angela Sunjakom comes from German heritage and also makes Hungarian goulash, Greek salads, Russian borsht, sloppy joes, and knockwurst. There's a good selection of German beers too.

◖ DENALI STATE PARK

This 325,240-acre state park (907/745-3975, www.alaskastateparks.org, $5/day trailhead parking) lies just southeast of Denali National Park and Preserve and is bisected by the Parks Highway from Mile 132 to Mile 169. Situated between the Talkeetna Mountains to the east and the Alaska Range to the west, the landscape of Denali State Park varies from wide glaciated valleys to alpine tundra. The Chulitna and Tokositna Rivers flow through western sections of the park, while the eastern half is dominated by Curry Ridge and Kesugi Ridge, a 35-mile-long section of alpine country.

Denali State Park provides an excellent alternative wilderness experience to the crowds and hassles of its federal next-door neighbor. The Mountain is visible from all over the park, bears are abundant, and you won't need to stand in line for a permit to hike or camp while you wait for Mount McKinley's mighty south face to show itself. Several trails offer a variety of hiking experiences and spectacular views.

Sights

Denali State Park is best known for its breathtaking **views of Mount McKinley** and the Alaska Range from pullouts along the Parks Highway. If The Mountain or even "just" some of the lower peaks of the Alaska Range are out, you won't need to read the next sentence to know what or where the sights are. The best viewpoint along the highway in the park, and the most popular, is at Mile 135, where on a clear day you will find an interpretive signboard and crowds of fellow travelers. Set up your tripod and shoot, shoot, shoot. Other unforgettable viewpoints are at Miles 147, 158, and 162.

The **Alaska Veterans Memorial** (Mile 147, within walking distance of Byers Lake Campground) consists of five monumental concrete blocks with stars carved out of them. Turn your back to the monument, and if you're lucky, there's blue-white McKinley, perfectly framed by tall spruce trees.

The western section of Denali State Park lies within the remote **Peters Hills,** an area known for its pristine Mount McKinley vistas and open country. This section is accessed via the Petersville Road.

Recreation

Little Coal Creek trailhead (Mile 164) is five miles south of the park's northern boundary. This is the park's gentlest climb to the alpine tundra—five miles east up the trail by Little Coal Creek, then you cut southwest along Kesugi Ridge, with amazing views of the Range and glaciers; flags and cairns delineate the trail. Watch for bears! The trail goes 27 miles until it hooks up with Troublesome Creek Trail just up from Byers Lake Campground. About halfway there, **Ermine Lake Trail** cuts back down to the highway, an escape route in case of really foul weather.

Troublesome Creek Trail is so named because of frequent bear encounters; in fact,

view of Mount McKinley and the Alaska Range from an overlook in Denali State Park

Troublesome Creek Trail is frequently closed in late summer and early fall because of the abundance of bears. It has two trailheads, one at the northeast tip of Byers Lake (Mile 147), the other at Mile 138. The park brochure describes this 15-mile hike along Troublesome Creek as moderate. It connects with Kesugi Ridge Trail just up from Byers Lake or descends to the easy five-mile **Byers Lake Loop Trail,** which brings you around to both campgrounds. Just down and across the road from the Byers Lake turnoff is a family day-hike along Lower Troublesome Creek—a gentle mile.

Based at Byers Lake, **Alaska Nature Guides** (907/733-1237, www.alaskanatureguides. com, mid-May-mid-Sept., 2.5-hour walks: $54 adults, $39 children; 5.5-hour hikes: $94 adults, $69 children) guides easy 2.5-hour nature walks and more interesting 5.5-hour hikes up Kesugi Ridge (includes lunch and gear). The guides are former national park rangers with years of local experience; the company also provides custom trips for birders and photographers.

Denali Southside River Guides (Byers Lake campground day-use parking lot, 907/733-7238, www.denaliriverguides.com) rents canoes and sit-on-top kayaks at Byers Lake. The company also leads full-day excursions ($249 adults, $179 kids) that combine kayaking, lunch, and rafting.

D&S Alaskan Trail Rides (Mile 133 Parks Hwy., 907/733-2207, www.alaskantrailrides. com, mid-May-late Sept.) has guided horseback rides from their location near Denali State Park. There are two-hour horseback rides ($119). Another option is a two-hour wagon ride with gold panning ($79). (The latter is primarily for cruise passengers staying at the nearby Mt. McKinley Princess Lodge.)

Accommodations

Turn off the highway at Mile 133 for a one-mile side road into **Mt. McKinley Princess**

Lodge (Mile 133 Parks Hwy., 907/733-2900 or 800/426-0500, www.princesslodges.com, mid-May-mid-Sept., $189-200 d). This stylish 460-room retreat is famous for its riverside location and picture-perfect vistas of the Alaska Range and Mount McKinley. Most rooms are filled with Princess cruise passengers, but anyone can stay or eat here. The lodge itself centers around a "great room" with a stone fireplace and enormous windows fronting the mountain. Lodging is in smaller buildings scattered around the grounds; ask for one of the new rooms with a king bed. There's also a small fitness center, two outdoor hot tubs, a restaurant, and a café. Wi-Fi is available only in the main lodge.

Located at the southern edge of Denali State Park, **Mary's McKinley View Lodge** (near Mile 134 Parks Hwy., 907/733-1555, www.mckinleyviewlodge.com, May-late Sept., $79-89 d) has a full service restaurant, great views of The Mountain out the big picture windows, and eight clean but older guest rooms with private baths. You can buy autographed copies of the many books authored by owner Jean Carey Richardson and her late mother, Mary Carey. There is no Wi-Fi here.

Camping and Cabins

Byers Lake Campground ($10) has large and uncrowded sites, water, outhouses, interpretive signs, and beautiful Byers Lake a stone's throw down the road. Also at Byers Lake are two popular **public-use cabins** (907/745-3975, www.alaskastateparks.org, $60). Just under two miles along the Loop Trail from the campground or across the lake by boat is **Lakeshore Campground,** with six primitive sites, outhouses, no running water, but unimpeded views of The Mountain and Range from your tent flap. Across the road and a quarter-mile south, **Lower Troublesome Creek Campground** ($10) has 20 sites and all the amenities of Byers Lake.

◖ DENALI HIGHWAY

The Denali Highway, which stretches 136 miles east-west across the waist of mainland Alaska from Cantwell, from 30 miles south of Denali Park to Paxson at Mile 122 on the Richardson

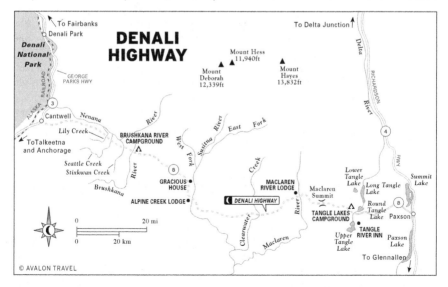

© AVALON TRAVEL

Highway, may be the best-kept secret in Alaska. Originally the Denali Highway was the only road into Denali National Park, and this beautiful side trip has been largely ignored by visitors since the opening of the George Parks Highway in 1971. Denali Highway is paved for 21 miles on the east end of the road (from Paxson to Tangle Lakes) and for three miles on the western end, but the rest is well-maintained gravel, which has received an undeserved bad rap—usually from folks hoping to set world land-speed records on their Alaska vacation.

The Denali Highway offers a varied selection of outstanding scenery and wildlife-viewing opportunities. Much of the route punches through the foothills of the magnificent Alaska Range. This area is part of the home range of the huge 30,000-strong Nelchina caribou herd. In the fall they begin to group in the greatest numbers—sightings of several hundred caribou are not unusual.

The Denali Highway is closed October-mid-May. In the winter it becomes a popular trail for snowmobilers, dog mushers, and cross-country skiers. Die-hard Alaskans also use this trail in the winter for access to unparalleled ice fishing and caribou and ptarmigan hunting.

As always, travelers on the Denali Highway should be prepared for emergencies. Always carry a spare tire and tire-changing tools, water, some snacks, and warm clothing. Towing is available from Paxson, Gracious House, and Cantwell, but it ain't cheap, so take your time and be safe.

History

The Denali Highway began as a "cat" track in the early 1950s when a man named Earl Butcher first established a hunting camp at Tangle Lakes. Known for years as Butcher's Camp, it's now the site of Tangle Lakes Lodge. About the same time, Chalmer Johnson established a camp at Round Tangle Lake. Now known as the Tangle River Inn, this lodge is still operated by the Johnson family.

Cantwell

A minuscule settlement (pop. 160) at the junction of the Parks Highway and Denali Highway, Cantwell began as a railroad settlement, and a cluster of decrepit buildings are strewn along the tracks two miles west of the highway. Cantwell is less than 30 miles south of Denali National Park, and a couple of businesses provide the staples: fuel, food, lodging, and booze. Most folks stop to fill up on the expensive gas, get a soda, and tool on up the highway. There aren't a lot of reasons to stay in Cantwell itself, though the surrounding country is grand.

Denali Sightseeing Safaris (Mile 188 Parks Hwy., 907/240-0357, www.denalisights.com, June-mid-Sept., seven-hour treks $160 adults, $80 children under 13) operates from the igloo on steroids 22 miles south of Cantwell. These unique tours are in customized big-tire trucks that allow them to cross glacial rivers and take you up old mining roads into the spectacular alpine area.

Cantwell Lodge (two miles off Parks Hwy., 907/388-8743, www.cantwellodgeak.com) houses a café, saloon, liquor store, laundry, showers, and Wi-Fi.

Also two miles from Parks Highway, **Blue Home B&B** (Caribou Ave., 907/768-2020, www.cantwell-bluehome.de, $130 d) has two spotless guest rooms that share a bath, full breakfasts, and Wi-Fi. The owners also speak German.

Bluesberry Inn (Mile 210 Parks Hwy., 907/768-2415, www.bluesberryinn.com, May-Nov., $75 d shared bath, $95-120 d private bath) provides reasonably priced—but very rustic—accommodations. There are dry cabins (they have electricity and heat, but no water) with a shared bathhouse and guest rooms with a double bed and private bath. Most units (except the dry cabins) have TV and Wi-Fi, and hostel-style bunks ($40 pp) may be available.

Backwoods Lodge (0.25 miles up Denali Hwy., 907/768-2231 or 800/292-2232, www.

© DON PITCHER

Denali Sightseeing Safaris operate from this igloo building south of Cantwell.

backwoodslodge.com, motel rooms $140-150 d, cabins $110-120 d) has clean, modern motel rooms with fridges, microwaves, TV, and Wi-Fi, and a pair of cabins. Motel rooms contain private baths, but the cabin guests use showers in the lodge.

Park RVs at **Cantwell RV Park** (an open lot near the junction with the Parks Hwy., 907/768-2210 or 800/940-2210, www.alaskaone.com/cantwellrv, mid-May-mid-Sept., tents $19, RVs $28-33). Services include Wi-Fi, showers, laundry, and a dump station.

EAST ON THE DENALI HIGHWAY

About three miles east of the Denali Highway-Parks Highway junction is a turnout with a view of Cantwell and Mount McKinley, if it's out. There's another potential view of the mountain at Mile 13, then in another five miles the highway runs parallel to the Nenana River. The headwaters of the Nenana emanate from a western digit of the ice fields atop the Alaska Range trio of peaks: **Mount Deborah** on the left at 12,339 feet, **Mount Hess** in the middle at 11,940 feet, and **Mount Hayes** on the right at 13,832 feet.

Over the next 10 miles the road crosses Lily Creek, Seattle Creek, and Stixkwan Creek; throw in a line and pull up some grayling or Dolly Varden. At Mile 31 you come to the **Brushkana River,** where the Bureau of Land Management (BLM) has a good free campground right on the river, and over the next 10 miles you get some great views of the three prominent peaks, along with the West Fork Glacier. The southern glaciers off Deborah, Hess, and Hayes feed the Susitna River, which flows west to the Parks Highway, and then south to empty into Cook Inlet across from Anchorage.

Gracious House Lodge and Beyond

Fifty-four miles east of the junction of the

Parks and Denali Highways is **Gracious House Lodge** (Mile 82 Denali Hwy., 907/333-3148, www.alaskaone.com/gracious, June-mid-Sept., guest rooms $135 d private bath; basic rooms $80 s, $105 d with access to showers; RVs $25, tents $15), a friendly mom-and-pop place where welcoming owners Butch and Carol Gratias have run things for more than 55 years. Guest rooms in the lodge are homey and clean and come with a private bath and light breakfast. Simple sleeping rooms come with access to the shower house. Park RVs or pitch a tent; both include showers. The owners can set up air-taxi and guide services, and provide minor tire and mechanical repairs or towing. Phone service into the lodge is via satellite phone, so it's generally best to make reservations through the email listed on their website. The lodge does, however, provide free Wi-Fi.

Five miles farther, you cross the single-lane 1,000-foot-long Susitna River bridge. Farther south, the Susitna is a popular river to float, but passage between here and there is considered impossible because of the impassable Devil's Canyon just downriver from the bridge.

Alpine Creek Lodge (Mile 68 Denali Hwy., 907/743-0565, www.alpinecreeklodge.com, lodge rooms $75 pp shared bath; suites $199 d private bath) has a beautiful setting for wilderness accommodations. Owners Claude and Jennifer Bondy operate this year-round place with reasonably priced lodging. There are 10 lodge rooms with bunk beds and a shared bath, as well as suites with private baths. Nearby are three small cabins ($30 pp for the two smaller cabins; $99 d for larger cabin, add $25 for extra guests) with woodstoves; guests use the bath in the lodge. The largest cabin sleeps up to six. A full breakfast is included in all rates, and hearty lunches and dinners are available. Summertime ATV tours are offered, along with fishing, hiking, and berry picking. In winter—when the lodge is only accessible by snowmobile—northern lights are the big attraction.

At Mile 79, the highway crosses Clearwater Creek; there are pit toilets at a rest stop and camping area here. In six miles is a turnout with a view of numerous lakes and ponds that provide a staging area for waterfowl; look for ducks, cranes, geese, trumpeter swans, and migrating shorebirds.

Maclaren

At Mile 93 out of Cantwell, the road crosses the Maclaren River, a tributary of the Susitna, flowing from the southern ice fields of mighty Mount Hayes. From here to the other end of the Denali Highway, you get occasional views of the three Alaska Range peaks. A mile west of the bridge is Maclaren River Road, which leads 12 miles north to Maclaren Glacier.

Just before the bridge crossing is **Maclaren River Lodge** (Mile 42 Denali Hwy., 907/822-5444, www.maclarenlodge.com, Feb.-Oct.), catering to hikers, hunters, anglers, and sightseers in the summer, and wintertime snowmobilers and dog teams. You can stay overnight in a duplex lodge ($150 for up to five people) with private baths, or in a separate lakeside cabin ($100 d) with a bathhouse. Other options include a pair of basic cabins with bunks ($25 pp), plus old Atco units ($60 d). The lodge has a relaxation area with satellite TV and Wi-Fi. A full-service restaurant (daily 7am-9pm, $10-30) serves burgers, steaks, seafood, and vegetarian specials, and the small bar has beer and wine. All sorts of day trips into the backcountry are offered. Especially popular are the jetboat trip to Maclaren Glacier ($65 pp), where you can camp near the glacier and then canoe back to the lodge.

In another seven miles is Maclaren Summit, at 4,080 feet the second-highest road pass in Alaska. It provides breathtaking views of Mount Hayes and the Maclaren Glacier. Peer through binoculars at the plains below to spot wildlife. Up at the summit you might see rock ptarmigan.

East End

The BLM's **Tangle Lakes Campground** (Mile 113, 907/822-3217, www.blm.gov/ak, free) has water pumps, pit toilets, blueberries in season, and a boat launch for extended canoe trips into the "tangle" (or maze) of lakes and ponds and creeks in the neighborhood.

One mile east of Tangle Lakes Campground is **Tangle River Inn** (Mile 114 Denali Hwy., 907/822-3970 summer or 907/892-4022 winter, www.tangleriverinn.com, mid-May-Sept.). Jack and Naidine Johnson have owned this classic Alaskan lodge since 1970; there's even a mountain named for Naidine nearby! The Johnsons sell gas, liquor, and gifts, and they offer good home cooking three meals a day (daily 7:30am-9pm), a lively bar with pool and foosball tables, simple lodging ($75 d shared bath, $100-150 d private bath), canoe rentals, and fishing gear.

The **Tangle Lakes Archaeological District** begins at Mile 119 and extends back to Crazy Notch at Mile 90. A short hike from the highway to any given promontory along this 30-mile stretch could have you standing at an ancient Athabascan hunting camp where no human footprints have been made for hundreds of years.

At Mile 122, there's a viewpoint from the summit that looks south over a great tundra plain. The three most prominent peaks of the Wrangell Mountains are visible from here: Mount Sanford on the left, Mount Drum on the right, and Mount Wrangell in the middle.

At Mile 125 is a paved turnout with a view of **Ten Mile Lake.** A short trail leads down to the lake, where you can catch grayling and trout. A turnout at Mile 129 affords a spectacular view of the Alaska Range to the north. The Gulkana and Gakona Glaciers can be seen from this point. The Denali Highway joins the Richardson Highway at Paxson.

Paxson

This tiny settlement at Mile 186 of the Richardson Highway and Mile 136 (from Cantwell) of the Denali Highway has two lodging options. **Paxson Lodge** (Mile 185.5 Richardson Hwy., 907/822-3330, www.paxson-lodge.com, $80 s, $100 d) offers gas, meals (daily 7am-9pm), and lodging, in rustic but clean rooms. There's a big deck for summertime dining three meals a day, a liquor store and bar, plus limited Wi-Fi.

Located just north of the highway junction, **Paxson Alpine Tours** (Mile 185.6 Richardson Hwy., 907/822-5972, www.denalihwy.com), guides birding hikes and rents bikes and kayaks. Owners Dr. Audie Bakewell and Jenny Rodina also operate **Denali Highway Cabins** ($160-200 d), with peaceful riverside cabins containing private baths, including a communal kitchen. Interested in glamping? Stay in one of the deluxe wall tents on riverside platforms ($160 d). A large guesthouse ($185 d, add $25 pp for extra guests; three-night minimum) with a full kitchen is also available. Guests have a continental breakfast basket delivered each morning, and guests have access to mountain bikes and the great room with a grand piano, games, and Wi-Fi.

Denali National Park and Preserve

Alaska's most famous tourist attraction, Denali National Park (907/683-2294, www.nps.gov/dena) draws over 400,000 visitors during its brief summer season. Most travelers come to see Mount McKinley, highest peak in North America (20,320 ft.), which towers above the surrounding lowlands and 14,000-17,000-foot peaks. Although it's visible only one day in three, and often shrouded for a week or more at a time, those who get lucky and see the mountain experience a thrill equivalent to its majesty and grandeur. Those who don't are usually consoled by lower snowcapped mountains and attending glaciers, high passes and adrenaline-pumping drops off the road, tundra vistas and "drunken forests," and an incredible abundance of wildlife, including caribou, moose, sheep, and bears. But even if the mountain is socked in, the grizzlies are hiding, and the shuttle-bus windows are fogged up, you're still smack in the middle of some of the most spectacular and accessible wilderness in the world. It was the call of the wild that brought you out here in the first place; all you have to do is step outside and answer.

THE LAND

The Alaska Range is a U-shaped chain that extends roughly 600 miles from the top of the Alaska Peninsula (at the head of the Aleutians) up through the park and down below Tok. It's only a small part, however, of the coastal mountains that include California's Sierra Nevada, the Northwest's Cascades, the Coast Mountains of British Columbia, Yukon's St. Elias Range, and eastern Alaska's Wrangell Range. The Park Road starts out a bit north of the Alaska Range and follows the U 90 miles southwest toward its heart—Mount McKinley. One thing that makes the mountain so spectacular is that the surrounding lowlands are so low: The entrance is at 1,700 feet, and the highest point on the road, Thoroughfare Pass, is just under 4,000 feet. The base of Mount McKinley is at 2,000 feet, and the north face rises at a 60-degree angle straight up to 20,000 feet—the highest vertical rise in the world.

Weather patterns here differ between the south side of the range (wetter and cooler) and the north. During the summer, the prevailing winds come from the south, carrying warm moisture from the Pacific. When they run smack into the icy rock wall of the Alaska Range, they climb, the moisture condenses,

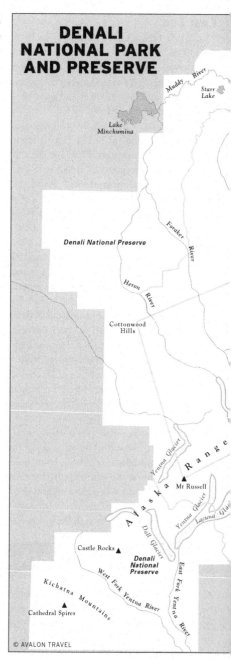

DENALI NATIONAL PARK AND PRESERVE

Muddy River
Starr Lake
Lake Minchumina
Denali National Preserve
Foraker River
Heron River
Cottonwood Hills
Range
Yentna Glacier
Mt Russell
Alaska
Yentna Glacier
Lacuna Glacier
Dall Glacier
Castle Rocks
Denali National Preserve
East Fork Yentna River
Kichatna Mountains
West Fork Yentna River
Cathedral Spires

© AVALON TRAVEL

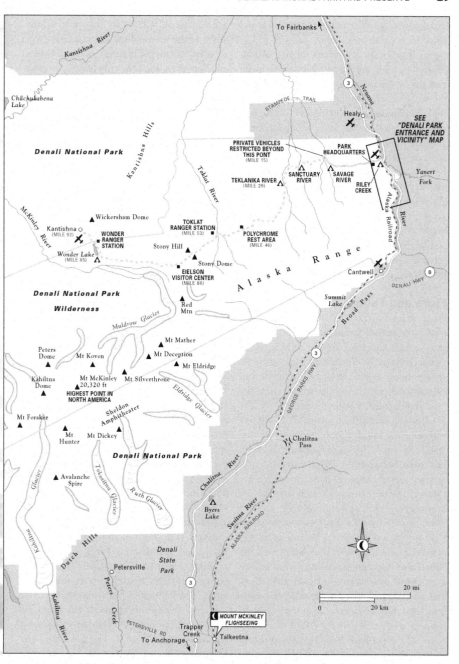

and depending on the amount of moisture and altitude, it either rains or snows—a lot. On top of that whole system sits mighty Mount McKinley, high, cold, and alone; it's so alone that the mountain has its own relationship to the weather. The combination of wind, wet, cold, and height creates extremely localized— and often violent—weather around Mount McKinley. Storms can blow in within an hour and last a week or more, dumping 10 feet of snow. Winds scream in at up to 80 mph. The mercury drops below zero in mid-July. Some of the worst weather in the world swirls around up there. But when the mountain emerges bright white against bright blue, and you're craning your neck to see the top, it's an unforgettable sight worth waiting around for—even in the rain.

Flora and Fauna

From sea level to around 2,300 feet is the habitat for the **boreal forest,** in which the black spruce, with its somber foliage and clusters of tawny cones, is the climax tree. Younger white spruce, along with deciduous aspen, birch, and cottonwood, grow near the streams and the road and in recently burned areas.

Climbing out of the forest above 2,300 feet you enter the **taiga,** a Russian word meaning "land of twigs." This transition zone (between the forest below and tundra above) accommodates no deciduous trees; the spruce are thinned out and runty (though they can be over 60 years old), and a green shag carpet of bush, mostly dwarf willow, layers the floor. Sitka spruce is the state tree because of its size, grandeur, and commercial value, but it's the willow that vegetates Alaska. And it has endless uses: Before synthetics like nylon, the willow bark was stripped, split, and braided and made into rope, bows, wicker baskets, snowshoes, fishnets, and small game and bird snares and traps. The inner bark is sweet; the sap is very sweet. Young buds and shoots are edible and

nourishing, and willows are the nearly exclusive staple of the moose diet. The taiga also hosts a variety of berries: blueberries and low-bush cranberries by the ton, crowberries, bearberries, soap and salmon berries, and raspberries.

Above 2,500 feet is the **tundra,** its name a Lapp word meaning "vast, rolling, treeless plain." There are two types of tundra: The moist, or Alaskan, tundra is characterized by the taiga's dwarf shrubbery, high grasses, and berries, but no trees; the alpine tundra, the highest zone, has grasses, moss, lichens, and small hardy wildflowers, including the stunning forget-me-not, Alaska's state flower.

The animal life varies with the vegetation. In the forest, look for moose, porcupine, snowshoe hare, marten, lynx, two kinds of weasels, red or tree squirrels, and several varieties of small rodents. On the taiga—or in both the forest and the tundra—you might see coyotes, wolves, foxes, grizzlies, and ground squirrels. In the tundra, keep an eye out for caribou, wolverines, Dall sheep, marmots, voles, lemmings, and shrews.

HISTORY

In 1896 a prospector named Bill Dickey was tramping around Interior Alaska looking for gold. Like everyone who sees it, Dickey was captivated by the size and magnificence of the mountain that was then variously known as Tenada, Denali, Densmore's Mountain, Traleika, and Bulshaia. Dickey was from Ohio, William McKinley's home state, and a Princeton graduate in economics. When he came out of the bush and heard that McKinley had been nominated for president, he promptly renamed the mountain "McKinley," wrote numerous articles for stateside magazines, and lobbied in Washington, D.C., in support of adoption of the name, which finally caught on after President McKinley was assassinated in 1901. The name has been something of a sore point with Alaskans ever

© DON PITCHER

Dall sheep

since, for McKinley had absolutely nothing to do with the mountain, and the more lyrical Native Alaskan names were completely ignored. Many in Alaska support renaming the peak Denali ("the high one"), a term used by Native Alaskans of the lower Yukon and Kuskokwim Rivers. Unfortunately, any move to eliminate "McKinley" from maps is inevitably met by howls of protest from Ohio's congressional delegation.

Creating a Park

Harry Karstens reached the Klondike in 1898 when he was 19, bored by Chicago and attracted by adventure and gold. Within a year he'd crossed over into U.S. territory and wound up at Seventymile, 20 miles south of Eagle. When the local mail carrier lost everything one night in a card game and committed suicide, Karstens took his place. He became proficient at dog mushing and trailblazing and within a few years was delivering mail on a primitive

trail between Eagle and Valdez, a 900-mile round-trip every month (the Richardson Highway follows the same route). Later he moved on to Fairbanks and began delivering mail to Kantishna, the mining town on what is now the west end of the park, growing very fond of and familiar with the north side of the Alaska Range. So when a naturalist from the East Coast, Charles Sheldon, arrived in 1906 to study Dall sheep in the area, Karstens guided him around Mount McKinley's northern foothills, delineating the habitat of the sheep. Karstens was also the co-leader of the four-man expedition that was the first party to successfully climb the true peak of Mount McKinley, the south summit, in 1913.

Meanwhile, Charles Sheldon was back in Washington, lobbying for national-park status for the Dall sheep habitat, and when Mount McKinley National Park was created in 1917, Karstens was the obvious choice to become the first park superintendent. He held that post in 1921-1928, patrolling the park boundaries by dogsled.

Woodrow Wilson signed the bill that created Mount McKinley National Park, Alaska's first, in 1917. The Park Road, begun five years later, was completed to Kantishna in 1940. In 1980, with the passage of the Alaska National Interest Lands Conservation Act, McKinley Park was renamed Denali National Park and Preserve and expanded to nearly six million acres, roughly the size of Vermont.

Pioneer Climbs

Many pioneers and prospectors had seen the mountain and approached it, but Alfred Brooks, a member of the first U.S. Geological Survey expedition in Alaska in 1902, was the first to set foot on it. He approached it from the south and reached an elevation of 7,500 feet before running out of time. He published an article in the January 1903 issue of *National Geographic* in which he recommended approaching the mountain from the north. Following that suggestion, the next attempt was from the north, led by James Wickersham, U.S. district judge for Alaska. Judge Wickersham was sent from Seattle to bring law and order to Eagle in 1900; he moved to Fairbanks in 1903. That summer, he had a spare couple of months and set out to climb the mountain, traveling more than 100 miles overland and reaching the 7,000-foot level of the north face, later named Wickersham Wall in honor of His Honor.

That same summer, Dr. Frederick Cook, who'd been with Peary's first party to attempt to reach the north pole in 1891 and Amundsen's Antarctic expedition of 1897, also attempted to climb the mountain from the north and reached 11,300 feet. In 1906, Cook returned to attempt Mount McKinley from the south, but he failed to get near it. His party broke up and went their separate directions, and a month later, Cook sent a telegram to New York claiming he'd reached the peak. This was immediately doubted by the members of his party, who challenged his photographic and cartographic "evidence." But through public lectures and articles, Cook's reputation as the first man to reach the peak grew. Two years later, he claimed to have reached the North Pole several months ahead of another Peary expedition, and Cook began to enjoy a cult status in the public consciousness. Simultaneously, however, his credibility among fellow explorers rapidly declined, and Cook vanished from sight. This further fueled the controversy and led to the Sourdough Expedition of 1910.

Four sourdoughs in Fairbanks simply decided to climb the mountain to validate or eviscerate Cook's published description of his route. They left town in December and climbed to the north peak in early April. The three members who'd actually reached the peak stayed in Kantishna to take care of business, while the fourth member, Tom Lloyd, who hadn't reached the peak, returned to Fairbanks and lied that he had. By the time the other three returned to town in June, Lloyd's story had already been published and widely discredited. So nobody believed the other three—*especially* when they claimed they'd climbed up to the north peak and down to their base camp at 11,000 feet in 18 hours, with a thermos of hot chocolate, four doughnuts, and dragging a 14-foot spruce log that they planted up top and claimed was still there. Finally, in 1913, the Hudson Stuck-Harry Karstens expedition reached the true summit, the south peak, and could prove that they'd done so beyond a shadow of a doubt. Only then was the Sourdough Expedition vindicated: All four members of the Stuck party saw the spruce pole still standing on the north peak!

Today more than 1,000 mountaineers attempt the summit of Mount McKinley each year, and approximately half of them actually reach the top. The youngest climbers ever to summit, a girl and a boy, were 12; the oldest man was 71, and the oldest woman 62.

PARK ENTRANCE

Pay the park admission ($10 pp) or buy a National Park Pass ($40 per year)—good for all national parks. A Senior Pass ($10) for all national parks is available to anyone over age 62 for a one-time fee, and people with disabilities can get a free Access Pass that covers all the parks. Get additional park information (907/683-2294, www.nps.gov/dena) by phone or online.

Planning Your Time

Denali National Park is open year-round, though most facilities only operate mid-May through mid-September. Plowing of the Park Road generally starts in early May, but only the first 30 miles are open before late May, when the shuttle buses begin running. Those who arrive before this date will not be able to reach the best vantage points for Mount McKinley.

The wildflowers peak around summer solstice—as do the mosquitoes. The berries, rose hips, and mushrooms are best in mid-August—as are the no-see-ums. The fall colors on the tundra are gorgeous around Labor Day weekend, when the crowds start to thin out and the northern lights start to appear, but it can get very cold. A skeleton winter Park Service crew patrols the park by dogsled. After the first heavy snowfall, the Park Road is plowed only to headquarters.

Visitor Centers

The **Denali Visitor Center** (Mile 1.2 Park Rd., daily 8am-6pm mid-May-mid-Sept.) is right across from the railroad depot. Step inside to explore the exhibits, get oriented from

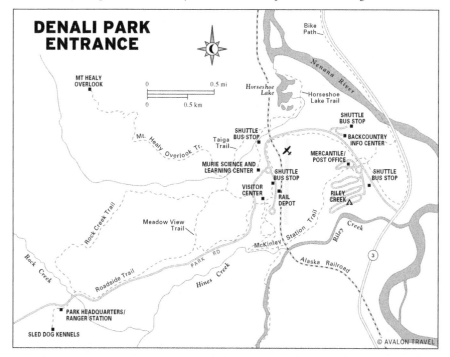

© AVALON TRAVEL

the enormous relief map of the park, talk with the rangers, and view an extraordinary 20-minute film, *Heartbeats of Denali*. Pick up a copy of *Denali Alpenglow*, the park newspaper, and check the bulletin board for a schedule of today's guided walks, talks, and kids' programs. Adjacent are an Alaska Natural History Association gift shop and Morino Grill, serving sandwiches, burgers, fish and chips, and pizzas.

On the other side of the traffic circle, the **Murie Science and Learning Center** (907/683-1269 or 888/688-1269, www.muriesclc.org) promotes scientific research and education through youth camps, field seminars, and courses in the summer. In the off-season—when other facilities are closed—the Murie building becomes the **winter park visitor center** (daily 9am-4pm winter). Check out the dinosaur track here that was found in the park.

Get park shuttle bus tickets and campground information at the **Wilderness Access Center** (daily 5am-8pm mid-May to mid-Sept.), located a half-mile up the Park Road. The reservations desk opens at 7am. While here you could also watch an 18-minute film about the park or buy snacks. This facility is run by the park concessionaire, Aramark.

Sled Dog Demonstrations

One of the highlights of the park is the sled dog demonstration (daily 10am, 2pm, and 4pm in peak season) at the kennels behind headquarters. The dogs are beautiful and accessible (the ones not behind fences are chosen for friendliness and patience with people), and the anxious collective howl they orchestrate when the lucky six dogs are selected to run is something to hear. Naturalists give a talk about the current and historical uses of dogs in the park, their breeding and training, different commands for controlling them, and the challenge of maintaining a working kennel in a national park. Then dogs are hitched up to a wheel sled and run around a gravel track. The enthusiasm of the dogs to get off the chain and into the harness is an eyebrow-raising glimpse into the consciousness of Alaskan sled dogs—they live to run.

A free shuttle bus leaves the Denali Visitor Center and the Riley Creek bus shelter 40 minutes before the demonstrations. Don't miss this one!

GETTING AROUND DENALI

In 1971, before the George Parks Highway connected McKinley National Park to Fairbanks (125 miles) and Anchorage (245 miles), you had to take the train, or from Fairbanks you had to drive down to Delta Junction, take the Richardson Highway to Paxson, the Denali Highway to Cantwell, then the Parks Highway up to the park entrance, for a grand total of 340 miles. From Anchorage you had to drive to Glennallen, then up the Richardson to Paxson, over to Cantwell and beyond, for 440 miles. That year, nearly 45,000 visitors passed through the park. In 1972, when the George Parks Highway radically reduced driving times from both main urban centers, almost 90,000 visitors came. In anticipation of the huge jump in tourism, the Park Service initiated the shuttle system of school buses running a regularly scheduled service along the Park Road. Today, the park sees 400,000 visitors annually.

◖ Denali Shuttle Bus Tours

There's no question that the shuttle system is highly beneficial to the park experience: The road is tricky and dangerous, crowds are much more easily controlled, there's much less impact on the wildlife (which take the buses for granted), and it's much easier to see wildlife when 40 passengers have eyeballs, binoculars, spotting scopes, and telephotos trained on the tundra. The excellent *Denali Road Guide*, available in park bookstores, has detailed information on sights along the road.

Green buses (daily mid-May-mid-Sept.) depart from the Wilderness Access Center, with some continuing all the way to the Kantishna, an exhausting 89-mile 13-hour round-trip ride. Most visitors don't go that far (or certainly not in one day), turning around instead at Polychrome Pass, Eielson, Wonder Lake, or other places along the way. Buses for Eielson begin departing from the Wilderness Access Center at 5am and continue roughly every 30 minutes through 3:30pm. Other buses depart during the day for Polychrome/Toklat and Wonder Lake.

You can reserve tickets in advance (907/272-7275 or 800/622-7275, www.reservedenali. com), starting in mid-February over the phone or on December 1 online, and up to the day before you travel. Sixty-five percent of the available tickets go on sale December 1; the other 35 percent are made available just two days ahead of the travel date. Adults pay $27 to Polychrome/Toklat (6 hours round-trip), $34 to Eielson (8 hours round-trip), $46 to Wonder Lake (11 hours round-trip), and $50 to Kantishna (12 hours round-trip). Kids under 15 ride free, and fares are half the adult price for children ages 15-17. Fares do not include park entrance fees ($10). Wheelchair-accessible shuttle buses are available. Backpackers pay $34 round-trip to anywhere in the park on the special **camper bus.**

It's recommended that you try to get on an early-morning bus into the park: There is a better chance to see wildlife and the mountain in the cool of the morning, and more time to get off the bus and fool around in the backcountry.

Schedules are readily available at the visitor centers and hotels. Take everything you need, as nothing (except books and postcards) is for sale once you get into the park. You can get off the bus and flag it down to get back on (if there's room; the buses leave with a few seats empty to pick up day-hikers in the park) anywhere along the road. Many riders never get off the bus at all and just stay on it for the entire exhausting round-trip.

Local Shuttles

A **Riley Creek Loop Bus** (5am-7pm mid-May-mid-Sept., free) provides service connecting the Riley Creek Campground, Wilderness Access Center, and train depot every half hour. In addition, a free bus connects the Wilderness Access Center with the dogsled demonstrations at park headquarters, and the free **Savage River Shuttle** provides service as far as Savage River Bridge at mile 15.

Private shuttle buses ($1-5) run among the train depot, Wilderness Access Center, and larger hotels, including Denali Bluffs Hotel, Grande Denali Lodge, McKinley Village Lodge, McKinley Chalet Resort, and Denali Princess Lodge. **Denali Salmon Bake** (www. denaliparksalmonbake.com, $1 each way, $2 to the Wilderness Access Center) provides a 24-hour shuttle that operates every 1.5 hours, stopping at the Wilderness Access Center, train depot, Denali Park/Canyon hotels and restaurants, and Healy businesses. The shuttle also stops at Riley Creek Campground upon request (call 907/683-2733 for a campground pickup).

Tour Buses

The park's **tan nature tour buses** (907/272-7275 or 800/622-7275, www.reservedenali. com) leave from the Wilderness Access Center throughout the day. For a good introduction, take a five-hour **Denali Natural History Tour** ($67 adults, $33 under age 15) to Primrose Ridge (17 miles each way), or for a better look, join the seven-hour **Tundra Wilderness Tour** ($113 adults, $57 under age 15, includes a box lunch) to Toklat, a distance of 53 miles each way. A shorter **Teklanika Tundra Wilderness Tour** ($74 adults, $37 kids) to Mile 30 may be offered in mid-May and mid-September if snow prevents access farther out the Park Road. **Kantishna Experience** ($159 adults, $80 under age 15, includes lunch) is a 12-hour tour that focuses both on wildlife and the history of this old gold mining town. All these tours are extremely popular, and fill up fast, so you need to make your reservations as far in advance as possible. **Kantishna Wilderness Trails** (907/683-8002 or 800/230-7275, www.denaliwildlifetour.com, $169 pp) provides private all-day bus tours that leave Denali Park hotels at 6:30am. These take you to Kantishna Roadhouse near the end of the road for a lunch, gold panning, and sled dog demonstration before heading back out, arriving at the hotels by 8pm. **Denali Backcountry Adventure** (866/900-1992, www.alaskadenalitours.com, $169 pp) provides all-day bus tours to Denali Backcountry Lodge in Kantishna. These 13-hour trips include lunch. Make it a fly/drive trip by flying back out on Kantishna Air (an additional $150).

Driving

For most of the summer, only the first 15 miles (to Savage River) of the Park Road are open to private vehicles. This portion is paved and makes for an excellent day trip. From early May, when the road is plowed, to late May, when the shuttle buses start running, it is possible to drive as far as the Teklanika River rest area at Mile 30. The road beyond this doesn't open until late May, so early park arrivals will not be able to see many of the sights for which it is famous.

At the end of summer, the Park Road is opened to auto traffic for four days in mid-September. Only 400 vehicles are allowed per day, and passes are selected by a lottery. In a typical year, you may be competing with 10,000 other entries for these passes! You'll need to apply during June; contact the **Park Service** (907/683-2294, www.nps.gov/dena) for details.

A handful of professional photographers are allowed vehicular access to the park during the summer, but these slots are highly sought after.

HEADING OUT ON THE PARK ROAD

A few miles beyond headquarters the road climbs out of the boreal forest, levels off, and travels due west through a good example of taiga. The ridgeline to the north (right) of the road is known as the **Outer Range,** foothills of the massive Alaska Range to the south (left). The Outer Range is much older, of different geological origins, and much more rounded and eroded than the jagged Alaska Range. The first view of the mountain comes up at Mile 9; look southwest. The day has to be nearly perfectly clear to see Mount McKinley from here: You're at around 2,400 feet, and the mountain is at 20,000 feet, which leaves nearly an 18-grand spread over 70-odd miles of potential cloud cover. That's a lot of potential.

Next you pass the Savage River Campground, then wind down to the river valley and cross the bridge that marks the end of road access for those in private vehicles. The "Checkpoint Charlie" kiosk at Mile 15 has a park employee to turn back private vehicles; they're prohibited beyond this point. From the bridge, look upriver (left) and notice the broad, U-shaped, glacial valley with large gravel deposits forming braids or channels, then look right to compare the V-shaped valley obviously cut by running water. The Savage Glacier petered out right where the bridge is now around 15,000 years ago during the last ice age. Here you also kiss the pavement good-bye, then start climbing Primrose Ridge, which offers excellent hiking, especially in June-early July when the wildflowers are in full bloom. Turn around and look back at the Savage Bridge; the stark rock outcropping just up from it has a distinct resemblance to an Indian's facial bone structure, which is how the Savage got its politically incorrect name. Just up the road is a pullout—if the mountain's out, the driver should stop for the clear shot.

Savage River to Igloo Canyon

Mount McKinley disappears behind jagged lower peaks as the road descends into the broad, glacial **Sanctuary River** valley at Mile

23. Watch for moose, caribou, foxes, lynx, waterfowl, and eagles along here. Right on the other side of the Sanctuary is a good view down at a "drunken forest," one effect that permafrost has on the vegetation. Notice how many of the trees are leaning at bizarre and precarious angles, with some of them down entirely. As an adaptation to the permafrost, these spruce trees have evolved a root system that spreads horizontally across the surface soil; there's no taproot to speak of. So the taller a tree grows around here, the less support it maintains, and the more susceptible it is to falling over. When the surface soil becomes saturated (because of lack of absorption over the permafrost), it sometimes shifts, either spontaneously or because of slight tremors (a major fault runs through here), taking the trees with it.

Next you descend into the broad **Teklanika River** valley, with a good view across the river of the three vegetation zones on the mountain slopes: forest, taiga, and tundra. You pass a number of small ponds in this area, known as "kettles," usually formed when a retreating glacier drops off a large block of ice, which melts, leaves a depression, and fills with rainwater. The stagnant water is rich in nutrients and provides excellent hatching grounds for Alaska's famous mosquitoes, and as such the ponds are good feeding spots for ducks and shorebirds. Look for mergansers, goldeneyes, sandpipers, buffleheads, and phalaropes in these ponds. And in some of the higher, smaller, more private kettles, look for hikers and park employees with no clothes on... maybe even join them, if you care to brave the skeeters, which have been known to show up on Park Service radar screens.

Cross the river and enter **Igloo Canyon,** where you turn almost due south. The mountain on the right is Igloo (4,800 ft.); the one on the left is Cathedral (4,905 ft.). Igloo is in the Outer Range, Cathedral in the Alaska Range. At the closest distance between the two ranges,

the canyon is right on the migration route of the Dall sheep and a great place to view them as white dots on the slopes; or climb either mountain to get closer.

Sable Pass (3,900 ft.) is next at Mile 38, the second-highest point on the road. This area is closed to hiking and photography because of the large grizzly population. Keep your eyes peeled. The next good views of the mountain are from these highlands.

Over Polychrome Pass to Eielson

Once you cross the **East Fork River** at Mile 44 (there is great hiking out onto the flats from here), you begin your ascent of Polychrome Pass, one of the most spectacular and fear-inducing sections of the road. If you're scared of heights or become frightened at the 1,000-foot drop-offs, just do what the driver does—close your eyes. These rocks have a high iron content; the rate of oxidation and the combination of the iron with other minerals determine the different shades of rust, orange, red, and purple. Look and listen for hoary marmots in the nearby rocks, and, from here almost the rest of the way to Eielson Visitor Center, watch for caribou and wolves; these are the Murie flats, where wildlife biologist Adolph Murie studied the lifestyle of *Canis lupus*.

Descend to the **Toklat River** at Mile 53, the last and largest you cross before Eielson. This is the terminus of the wildlife tour, but the shuttle buses continue on to Eielson and Wonder Lake. The Toklat's source is the Sunrise Glacier, just around the bend upriver (left). You can see from the size of the river how big the glacier was 20,000 years ago. There is great hiking up into the Alaska Range from here. Next you climb up **Stony Hill** and, if the weather is cooperating, when you crest the ridge you're in for the thrill of a lifetime: Denali, The Great One, in all its immense majestic glory. It's hard to believe that the mountain is still 40 miles away! But wait, you get another five miles closer, crossing

Thorofare Pass (3,950 ft.), the highest elevation on the road, at Mile 62.

◖ Eielson Visitor Center

Eielson Visitor Center (daily 9am-7pm June-mid-Sept.) is four hours and 66 miles from the park entrance. The view from here—weather cooperating—is unforgettable. Even if you can only see the bottom 12,000-14,000 feet, have a naturalist or your driver point to where the top of Mount McKinley is, and visualize it in your mind's eye. Also, things change fast around here, so keep an eye out for the peak popping out of the clouds as a surprise just for you.

The earth-friendly visitor center at Eielson opened in 2008, featuring exhibits, tall windows facing McKinley, short-term lockers, an outdoor deck, 24-hour bathrooms, and space to enjoy your lunch or relax. Check out the interlocked moose antlers out front; the two bulls died when they sparred and their antlers became locked together.

Naturalists lead 45-minute walks (daily 1pm). The excellent backpacking zones in this area are usually the first to fill up. There's nothing for sale at Eielson, so be sure to bring food and any needed maps or books.

◖ Wonder Lake

Beyond Eielson, the road comes within 25 miles of the mountain, passing **Muldrow Glacier,** which is covered by a thick black layer of glacial till and vegetation. From Wonder Lake, the **Wickersham Wall** rises magnificently above the intervening plains, with the whole Alaska Range stretching out on each side. In addition, the reflection from the lake doubles your pleasure and doubles your fun, from which even the mosquitoes here, some of the most savage, bloodthirsty, insatiable beasts of the realm, cannot detract.

There's a popular campground at Wonder Lake (Mile 85), and a nearby pond is where those postcard-perfect moose-in-the-lake-with-Mount-McKinley photos are taken. Many buses turn around at Wonder Lake, but a few continue to Kantishna.

Kantishna

The town of Kantishna, 92 miles from the park entrance at the western end of the Park Road, has five roadhouses. The area was first settled in 1905, when several thousand miners rushed to the foothills just north of Mount McKinley to mine gold, silver, lead, zinc, and antimony. After 1980 and the Alaska National Interest Lands Conservation Act, which expanded Denali National Park's boundaries, Kantishna found itself inside the park, and in 1985 mining was halted by court order. The road ends at the last lodge, where buses turn around to return to the park entrance. An air taxi is based here, and most Kantishna lodges have their own shuttle buses and tours.

DAY HIKES

Ranger-led walks are available daily all summer at both the Denali Visitor Center and Eielson Visitor Center. More ambitious are the half-day **Discovery Hikes** ($34 adults, free kids under 15) led by rangers to more remote areas. These include several hours on the bus en route to your starting point; reserve a day or two in advance at the Wilderness Access Center (daily 5am-8pm mid-May to mid-Sept.).

Note: Guns are now legally permitted within Denali National Park, but they aren't allowed on most shuttle and tour buses. Research indicates that hikers carrying guns are more likely to be injured in bear attacks than those who carry pepper-based bear sprays such as Counter Assault. There has only been one fatal bear attack in the park (in 2012), but bears certainly are a potential hazard. Be sure to carry bear spray, and have it accessible.

Entrance Area Hikes

Several paths take off from the Denali Visitor

Mount McKinley vista from Wonder Lake

©DON PITCHER

Center, including two easy ones: the **Spruce Forest Trail** (15 minutes) and a slightly longer **Murie Science and Learning Center Trail** (20 minutes). **Horseshoe Lake Trail** (three miles round-trip) starts at the shuttle bus stop and then descends to the lake, where you might see waterfowl and beavers.

Hiking the five-mile round-trip **Mount Healy Overlook Trail** is a great way to get the lay of the land, see the mountain if it's out, quickly leave the crowds behind, and get your heart pumping. Once at the overlook (one mile in), keep climbing the ridges for another several hours to get to the peak of Mount Healy (5,200 ft.).

The 2.3-mile **Rock Creek Trail** starts near the post office and climbs to park headquarters, gaining 400 feet along the way. You can then loop back along the road via the 1.8-mile **Roadside Trail.** The **Taiga Trail** is an easy 1.3-mile loop that also begins near the post office.

Eielson Hikes

The Eielson Visitor Center at Mile 66 is located in open tundra, with Mount McKinley and other Alaska Range peaks dominating southern vistas. Just downhill from Eielson is the 0.8-miles **Tundra Loop Trail,** a good place to stretch your legs after the four-hour bus ride from the park entrance. Look for wildflowers and arctic ground squirrels along the way. A spur leads to a knoll overlooking the valley, and across the road from Eielson is an even shorter loop path for a quick jaunt before settling back into your bus.

The **Alpine Trail** is considerably more strenuous, climbing steeply up Thorofare Ridge, which looms above Eielson Visitor Center. It's 2.2 miles each way, with a gain of 1,000 feet in elevation as you hike a series of switchbacks and rock steps. Stop along the way to take in the view. The summit (almost 5,000 feet in elevation) is wide and flat with views in all directions. Grizzly bears and caribou are often

COEXISTING WITH BEARS

© DON PITCHER

Bears seem to bring out conflicting emotions in people. The first is an almost gut reaction of fear and trepidation: What if the bear attacks me? But then comes that other urge: What will my friends say when they see these *incredible* bear photos? Both of these reactions can lead to problems in bear country. "Bearanoia" is a justifiable fear, but it can easily be taken to such an extreme that one avoids going outdoors at all for fear of running into a bear. The "I want to get close-up shots of that bear and her cubs" attitude can lead to a bear attack. The middle ground incorporates a knowledge of and respect for bears with a sense of caution that keeps you alert for danger without letting fear rule your wilderness travels. Nothing is ever completely safe in this world, but with care you can avoid most of the common pitfalls that lead to bear encounters.

Both brown (grizzly) and black bears occur throughout Southcentral Alaska. Old-timers joke that bears are easy to differentiate: A black bear climbs up the tree after you, while a grizzly snaps the tree off at the base. Both grizzlies and black bears pose potential threats to backcountry travelers.

Enter bear country with respect but not fear. Bears rarely attack humans; you're a thousand times more likely to be injured in a highway accident than by a bear. In fact, more people in Alaska are hurt each year by moose or dogs than by bears. Contrary to the stories you often hear, bears have good eyesight, but they depend more upon their excellent senses of smell and hearing. A bear can tell who has walked through an area, and how recently, with just a quick sniff of the air. Most bears hear or smell you long before you realize their presence, and they hightail it away.

Bears are beautiful, eminently fascinating, and surprisingly intelligent animals. They can be funny, playful and inquisitive, vicious or protective, and unpredictable. The more you watch bears in the wild, the more complex their lives seem, and the more they become individual animals, not simply the big and bad.

spotted along the way. Return the same way, and plan on two hours round-trip. This hike is one of the popular ranger-led Discovery Hikes offered daily at noon in the summer. Make reservations at Eielson (daily 9am-7pm June-mid-Sept.), but get here early to reserve your place for this memorable hike (maximum of 11 people).

Wonder Lake Hikes

The open country around Wonder Lake Campground provides relatively easy hiking, or walk up the road to Reflection Pond and the outlet to Wonder Lake. The only trail in the area is the **McKinley Bar Trail,** an easy five-mile round-trip hike from the campground. The trail passes through open country with small ponds, bogs, and creeks before cutting through spruce forests to the McKinley River. The braided river changes channels constantly, with easy hiking opportunities on the open mile-wide river bar with Denali providing a magnificent backdrop. Do not attempt to cross this large glacier-fed river with deep, fast-flowing water. The area is plagued by mosquitos much of the summer, so bring a head net and bug dope.

Guided Hikes

Denali Backcountry Guides (907/683-4453, www.walkdenali.com, mid-May-mid-Sept.) offers two unique ways to explore the country just outside the park. Seven-hour pack rafting trips ($199 pp) are tailored to your abilities, providing time on a local river plus hiking; cost includes dry suits and transport. Also popular are four-hour heli-hiking wildlife walks ($475 pp) that include a helicopter flight to the high country followed by a hike. The company also leads three-hour natural history walks ($109 pp) in the Healy area for cruise ship folks.

BACKCOUNTRY TRIPS

For details on backcountry hikes and camping, head to the **Backcountry Information Center** (across the parking lot from the Wilderness Access Center, 907/683-9510, daily 9am-6pm May 20-Sept. 20).

Popular backpacking areas include up the Savage River toward Fang Mountain; down the far side of Cathedral Mountain toward Calico Creek (get off the bus just before the Sable Pass closure); up Tatler Creek a little past Igloo Mountain; anywhere on the East Fork flats below Polychrome toward the Alaska Range; anywhere around Stony Hill; and the circumnavigation of Mount Eielson (get off 5-6 miles past the visitor center, cross the 100 braids of the Thorofare River, and walk around the mountain, coming back up to the visitor center). There are backcountry description guides at the backcountry desk, or you can find the same info online, with photos.

On all these hikes, you can get off the outbound bus, explore to your heart's content, then get back on an inbound bus, if space is available. Consult with the driver and study the bus schedule closely; the camper buses may have space coming back.

Large as it is, it's hard to get lost in Denali—you're either north or south of the road. And since the road travels mostly through open alpine tundra, there aren't any artificial trails to follow—just pick a direction and go. Usually you'll want to make for higher ground in order to get out of the knee-to hip-high dwarf shrubbery of the moist tundra and onto the easy hiking of the alpine area, get to where the breeze will keep the skeeters at bay, and see more. Or walk along the river gravel bars into the mountains, although depending on the size of the gravel, it can be ankle-twisting. Hiking boots are a must, and carry food, water, a compass, binoculars, maps, rain gear, and a bear-proof food canister. Keep your eyes and ears wide open for wildlife that you don't want to get close to, sneak up on, or be surprised by.

© DON PITCHER

ranger giving a talk at Wonder Lake

Backcountry Permits

You need a free permit to spend the night in the backcountry. Permits are issued 24 hours in advance from the Backcountry Information Center, and reservations are not accepted. Check the big maps and look over descriptions of the 43 units, where a limited number of backpackers are allowed. (The same information can be found online at www.nps.gov/dena to help you plan prior to your trip.) Now check the board to find the vacancies in the units. Make sure the unit is open (some are always closed; others periodically close because of overcrowding or bears) and that there are enough vacancies to accommodate your whole party. Watch the 30-minute backcountry video that describes bear safety, river crossings, minimum-impact camping, emergencies, and other topics; listen to a 10-minute safety talk; and finally get a permit from the ranger. You might have to wait a few days for openings in your chosen area, or have a plan B or C in mind. The

park loans out free bear-proof food storage containers; be sure to get one for your hike. Finally, reserve a seat on one of the camper buses ($33) to get you and your gear into the park.

OTHER RECREATION
Mountain Biking

An excellent way to explore Denali at your own pace is by mountain bike. Bikes are allowed on the Park Road, and can be transported aboard the camper shuttle bus, but be sure to mention the bike when you make a reservation. Note that only camper buses carry bikes and that they only carry two at a time, so it is possible to get far out on the Park Road and then find yourself unable to catch a bus back. Be sure to pick up a "rules of the road" handout at the visitor center before heading out.

Denali Outdoor Center (907/683-1925 or 888/303-1925, www.denalioutdoorcenter.com, bike rental: $25/half-day, $40 for 24 hours) has mountain bike rentals and tours. Two-hour

PROTECTING YOURSELF DURING A BEAR ENCOUNTER

If you happen to encounter a bear, stay calm and don't make any sudden moves. Do not run: Bears can exceed 40 miles per hour for short distances. Don't climb a tree, as it may actually incite an attack. Instead, make yourself visible by moving into the open so the bear will identify you as a human and not something to eat. Never stare directly at a bear. Dropping an item such as a hat or jacket may distract the bear, and talking calmly also seems to have some value in convincing bears that you're a human. If the bear sniffs the air or stands on its hind legs, it is probably trying to identify you. When it does, it will usually run away. If a bear woofs and postures, don't imitate—this is a challenge. Keep retreating. Most bear charges are also bluffs; the bear will often stop short and amble off.

If a **grizzly bear** attacks, freeze. It may well be a bluff charge, with the bear halting at the last second. If the bear does not stop its attack, use bear spray immediately. If the bear is going to make contact, curl up facedown on the ground in a fetal position with your hands wrapped behind your neck and your elbows tucked over your face. Your backpack may help protect you. Remain still even if you are attacked, because sudden movements may incite further attacks. Often a bear will only sniff or nip you and leave. The injury you might sustain would be far less than if you tried to resist. After the attack, prevent further attacks by staying down on the ground until the grizzly has left the area. Do not play dead if the bear is at a distance or is leaving the area.

Bear authorities recommend against dropping to the ground if you are attacked by a **black bear,** because they tend to be more aggressive in such situations and are more likely to prey on humans. If a black bear attacks, use bear spray immediately. If you don't have the spray, fight back with whatever weapons are at hand; large rocks and branches can be effective deterrents, as can yelling and shouting. Aim for sensitive areas such as the bear's eyes or nose. Have a park ranger explain the difference between brown and black bears before you head into the backcountry.

Nighttime bear attacks could happen to even the most seasoned adventurer. In the rare event of a night attack in your tent, defend yourself very aggressively. Never play dead under such circumstances. Before going to bed, try to plan escape routes, and be sure to have a flashlight and pepper spray handy. Keeping your sleeping bag partly unzipped also allows the chance to escape should a bear attempt to drag you away. There are advantages to having multiple tents in case one person is attacked, and if someone is attacked in a tent near you, yelling and throwing rocks or sticks may drive the bear away.

A relatively recent development for campers in bear country is the use of portable **electric fences** made by Electro Bear Guard (907/562-2331, www.electrobearguard.com) to surround your campsite; a backpacker unit runs on two AA batteries, weighs just 2.5 pounds, and costs $395.

Cayenne pepper sprays ($35-50) such as Counter Assault (800/695-3394, www.counterassault.com) can be useful in fending off bear attacks, and experts recommend that hikers in bear country carry a can. They're sold in most Alaskan camping supply stores.

These sprays are effective only at close range (10-30 feet), particularly in tundra areas, where winds quickly disperse the spray. When you carry pepper spray, make sure it is readily available by carrying it in a holster on your belt or across your chest. Be sure to test-fire it to make sure you are comfortable using it. If you use the spray to drive a bear away, immediately leave the area since the bear may return. When carrying the spray, be sure the safety clip remains in place so it doesn't accidentally discharge.

Detailed bear safety brochures are available at the Alaska Public Lands Information Center (www.alaskacenters.gov) in Anchorage, or on the Alaska Department of Fish and Game's website (www.adfg.state.ak.us). Two good bear safety books are *Bear Attacks: Their Causes and Avoidance* by Stephen Herrero and *Bear Aware: Hiking and Camping in Bear Country* by Bill Schneider.

© DON PITCHER

mountain bikers in Denali National Park

bike tours (from $50 pp) have a minimum of four riders. Their office is eight miles north of Denali Park and two miles south of Healy, with a free shuttle provided.

Rafting

Three raft companies run the Nenana River along the eastern margin of the park, including two-hour Class II-IV white-water trips or Class II-III float trips ($90): **Denali Outdoor Center** (907/683-1925 or 888/303-1925, www.denalioutdoorcenter.com), **Denali Raft Adventures** (907/683-2234 or 888/683-2234, www.denaliraft.com), and **Nenana Raft Adventures** (907/683-7238 or 800/789-7238, www.raftdenali.com). All provide rain gear, boots, and life jackets, plus transportation to and from local hotels. Denali Raft Adventures and Denali Outdoor Center also offer trips that combine both segments for a four-hour trip ($122) that includes both the rapids and easy sections of the river.

Other Denali Raft Adventures options

include a four-hour scenic float ($142) and an all-day trip that includes floating and rapids ($183). Denali Outdoor Center has five-hour whitewater and scenic trips ($117 adults, $57 kids) and all-day 30-mile trips down the Nenana River ($173 adults, $153 kids). Float trips are okay for children, but only adults can do the white-water runs. Denali Outdoor Center would be my first choice, and they also provide inflatable kayak tours for those who want to paddle on their own.

Flightseeing

If the mountain is out and there's room on the plane, this is the time to pull out the credit card. These one-hour flights around Mount McKinley will leave you flying high for days.

Denali Air (Mile 229 Parks Hwy., 907/683-2261, www.denaliair.com, one-hour trip $375) operates from a private airstrip (eight miles south of the park entrance). Their one-hour trip over the mountain is in a twin-engine plane.

©DON PITCHER

Mount McKinley, as seen from a flightseeing trip over the park

Operating from Healy—12 miles north of the park entrance—**Fly Denali** (a.k.a. Talkeetna Aero Services, Healy River State Airport, 907/683-2899 or 888/733-2899, www.talkeetnaaero.com, $449 pp) has 2.5-hour flights that include a glacier landing.

Based in Kantishna at the center of the park, **Kantishna Air Taxi** (907/644-8222, www.katair.com) provides charter air service to end-of-the-road Kantishna lodges, and flightseeing trips within the park. Quite a few other flightseeing companies operate out of Talkeetna and Anchorage.

You can go for a helicopter ride on **Era Helicopters** (907/683-2574 or 800/843-1947, www.eraflightseeing.com), based along the river in Denali Park. Tour options include a 60-minute flight over the park ($339 pp), a 75-minute trip that includes a 20-minute glacier landing ($439), and a heli-hiking adventure that includes a 15-minute flight plus 3.5 hours of hiking ($475).

Mountaineering

Mount McKinley—the tallest peak in North America—is a major destination for mountaineers from around the globe. Over 1,000 climbers attempt to summit Mount McKinley each year, with three-quarters of these attempts via the West Buttress. The primary climbing season is May-July. From the south side of Mount McKinley, the usual approach is by ski plane from Talkeetna to the Southeast Fork of the Kahiltna Glacier or to the Ruth Glacier in the Don Sheldon Amphitheater. From the north, the approach for Denali and other peaks is by foot, ski, or dogsled. Specific route information can be obtained from the Talkeetna Ranger Station. Climbers on Mount McKinley and Mount Foraker are charged a special use fee ($350 per climber). Call the ranger in Talkeetna (907/733-2231), or visit the Park Service website (www.nps.gov/dena) for additional mountaineering information.

Six companies are authorized to lead guided

mountaineering climbs of Mount McKinley and other peaks in the Alaska Range; contact the Park Service for specifics. One of the finest is **Alaska Mountaineering School** (headquarters at 3rd St. and D St., Talkeetna, 907/733-1016, www.climbalaska.org, late Apr.-mid-July, 21-day climb $6,400 pp). The company guides 21-day climbs of the West Buttress with six climbers and two or three guides. These depart every week (or more often). The school also teaches intensive mountaineering courses, skills workshops, wilderness first responder classes, glacier treks, and wilderness backpacking. Another recommended climbing program is **NOLS** (907/745-4047, www.nols.edu), based in Palmer.

Dog Mushing

Visitors whose appetite is whetted by the daily dogsledding demonstrations at park headquarters may want to return when the snow flies for the real thing. **Earth Song Lodge** (Stampede Rd., 907/683-2863, www.earthsonglodge.com) offers wintertime dogsled adventure tours into Denali National Park. These range from an easy overnight trip to ones lasting 10 days.

Four-time Iditarod winner Jeff King lives with his family at Goose Lake near Denali, and his staff offers summertime tours of his state-of-the-art **Husky Homestead** (907/683-2904, www.huskyhomestead.com, 2.5 hour tours $59 adults, $39 children) kennels and training area. Tours and demonstrations depart from local hotels. It's by far the most tourist-oriented dog tour you'll ever see, handling almost 100 people at a time on busy summer days.

ENTERTAINMENT AND EVENTS

All the Denali Park hotels have lounges, but if you want to hang out with the young working crowd, head to **Denali Salmon Bake** (Mile 238.5 Parks Hwy., 907/683-2733, www.denaliparksalmonbake.com, daily 7am-11pm mid-May-late Sept.). For frivolity, check out **Alaska Cabin Nite Dinner Theater** (McKinley Chalet Resort, 907/276-7234 or 800/276-7234, www.denaliparkresorts.com) or the **Music of Denali Dinner Theater** (Denali Princess Lodge, 907/683-2282 or 800/426-0500, www.princesslodges.com).

Park Service rangers give talks, walks, and kid programs. For specifics, check the bulletin boards at the Denali Visitor Center or the free park newspaper, **Denali Alpenglow**.

SHOPPING

Denali Park's "Glitter Gulch" area is filled with gift shops, most of which are completely forgettable. Two good seasonal places for Alaskan art on the boardwalk are **Denali Glass Studio** (Mile 238.5 Parks Hwy., 907/683-2787) and **Three Bears Gallery** (Mile 238 Parks Hwy., 907/683-3343). Get quality outdoor gear, freeze dried food, and clothing at **Denali Mountain Works** (907/683-1542, www.akrivers.com), where you'll also find rental tents, packs, sleeping pads, stoves, and binoculars. It's a good place for that last-minute item you forgot.

There's a seasonal **farmers market** (parking lot of 229 Parks Restaurant, Mile 229 Parks Hwy., Sat. 10am-2pm) with local crafts and produce.

ACCOMMODATIONS

Most of the local lodging action centers around busy Denali Park, though other lodges and B&Bs are a few miles south of the park entrance, or 10 miles north in the town of Healy. Denali area lodging options are expensive, so those on a tight budget will either need to camp or head to the hostel 13 miles south at Carlo Creek.

Denali Park Lodging

If you've been driving the Parks Highway north from Anchorage, soaking up the wild Alaskan wilderness, you're in for a rude awakening

© DON PITCHER

"Glitter Gulch" shops near the entrance to Denali National Park

when you reach the unincorporated settlement called—take your pick—**"The Canyon," Denali, Denali Park,** or **"Glitter Gulch."** Just a mile north of the Denali National Park turn-off, it's impossible to miss: an ugly hodgepodge of giant hotels, restaurants, RV parks, rafting companies, and gift shops crammed between the highway and the Nenana River to the west, and climbing the steep hillside to the east. The area is packed with tour buses, tottering tourists, and rumbling RVs.

Most lodging choices start well over $200 per night, but one place offers a less-expensive option: **Denali Salmon Bake Cabins** (Mile 238.5 Parks Hwy., 907/683-2733, www.denali-nationalparklodging.net, early May-late Sept., $64 d shared bath, $145 d private bath, suite $269). For the full-on Alaskan experience, stay in a "hostel style cabin" consisting of insulated tent-like structures with two double beds and a shared bath. There are also four standard cabins with two full beds, private baths, cable TV,

fridges, and air-conditioning. It's not for everyone, but the "Bake" is right there in the thick of things near the park entrance, with free Wi-Fi. Also available is a large luxury suite that sleeps up to six and has a king bed, two futons, two TVs, a full kitchen, and bath. It's located atop Sled Dog Market. Reservations are advised.

Denali Bluffs Hotel (Mile 238 Parks Hwy., 907/683-8500 or 866/683-8500, www.denalialaska.com, late May-mid-Sept., $199 d) is a pleasant hillside place where 112 rooms all contain two doubles or one king bed. Request a room with a private balcony. High atop the bluff sits **Grande Denali Lodge** (Mile 238 Parks Hwy., 907/683-8500 or 866/683-8500, www.denalialaska.com, late May-mid-Sept., guest rooms $279 d, cabins $329 for up to four), a 166-room hotel accessed by a steep switchbacking road marked by amusing signs. Guests stay in spacious rooms or family style cabins. Both Denali Bluffs and Grande Denali have the same Native Alaskan management. There is a free shuttle to the park visitor center or a ride ($4) to the train depot.

Also managed by Aramark, **McKinley Chalet Resort** (Mile 236 Parks Hwy., 907/276-7234 or 800/276-7234, www.denaliparkresorts.com, mid-May-mid-Sept., $299-334 d, rooms with a view $369 d) is a 345-room hotel along the Nenana River. Most rooms are set aside for Holland America passengers, so call well ahead of your visit. Standard rooms are very overpriced.

Though primarily for cruise ship passengers, the sprawling **Denali Princess Lodge** (Mile 238 Parks Hwy., 907/683-2282 or 800/426-0500, www.princesslodges.com, mid-May-mid-Sept., $299 d) is also open to independent travelers if they don't mind the corporate feeling and constant parade of tour buses. There are 656 rooms, and so many buildings here that you'll need a map to find your way around. Amenities include outdoor hot tubs overlooking the Nenana River, a fitness center, restaurants and cafés, a dinner theater, and a bar.

On the east side of the road, **Denali Rainbow Village** (Mile 238.6 Parks Hwy., 907/683-7777, www.denalirv.com, mid-May-mid-Sept., $125 d) has a handful of motel rooms, each with a queen bed, kitchenette, private bath, and Wi-Fi.

Carlo Creek Area Lodging

A number of lodging places are in the Carlo Creek area near Mile 224 of the Parks Highway, 14 miles south of the park entrance. The least expensive is the friendly **Denali Mountain Morning Hostel and Lodge** (Mile 224.1 Parks Hwy., 907/683-7503, www.denalihostel.com, early May-late Sept.), with a variety of earthy creek-side accommodations: coed bunk cabins ($32 pp), a private room ($85 d), two-person cabins ($80-95 d; add $15 pp for additional adults), family cabins ($128-160 for up to five), and wall tents ($32 s, $55 d). There's a two-night minimum

stay in the private accommodations. A shower house and bathrooms are separate, and guests can use the central kitchen, computer, laundry, free Wi-Fi, and lounge. Rent bear spray and binoculars if you're heading into the park. Two good restaurants—Pizza Panorama and McKinley Creekside Café—are directly across the highway. The hostel provides a free four-times-daily shuttle to Denali's Wilderness Access Center.

Denali Perch Resort (Mile 224 Parks Hwy., 907/683-2523 or 888/322-2523, www.denaliperchresort.com, mid-May-mid-Sept., $85 d shared bath, $125 d private bath) has 20 tiny hillside cabins with a shared bathhouse or with Lilliputian private baths and Wi-Fi. There are no phones or TVs, but a good restaurant is on the premises, with two more just down the way.

Nearby is **Carlo Creek Lodge** (Mile 224 Parks Hwy., 907/683-2576, www.denaliparklodging.com, late May-early Sept., $84-90 d shared bath, $120-140 d private bath, motel rooms $120-130 d), which has 10 attractive cabins near the creek; some contain kitchens. In addition to cabins, there are a half-dozen motel rooms with queen beds. All units include microwaves, fridges, Wi-Fi, and guest computers.

Best known for its popular café, **McKinley Creekside Cabins & Café** (Mile 224 Parks Hwy., 907/683-2277 or 888/533-6254, www.mckinleycabins.com, $139-189 d, house $449) has a variety of rooms and cabins, along with a custom three-bedroom house. Wi-Fi is available.

Denali Cabins (907/683-2643 or 800/808-8068, www.denali-cabins.com, $159 d one double bed, $189 d two double beds, add $20 pp for extra guests) consists of 45 basic cedar cabins seven miles south of the park entrance. There is no Wi-Fi, but the cabins—connected by boardwalks—include phones, TVs, and private baths. A free shuttle to the park train station is provided, and guests can use the two hot tubs. Also here is restaurant (Prey Bar &

© DON PITCHER

Grande Denali Lodge, near the entrance to Denali National Park

Eatery) with pub fare. Alaska Denali Tours owns these cabins, and offers park day trips on their buses.

Across the highway is **Denali Grizzly Bear Resort** (Mile 231.1 Parks Hwy., 907/683-2696 or 866/583-2696, www.denaligrizzlybear.com, mid-May-mid-Sept.), with a range of lodging choices sprawling up the hillside. These include simple little cabins ($69-109 d), some of which use a central shower house, and attractive log cabins with private baths and kitchens ($199-269 for up to six people). Traffic noise can be an annoyance. Four new hotel buildings ($199 d) each have a private deck overlooking the Nenana River, private baths, and a continental breakfast. There is free Wi-Fi throughout the resort, and a guest laundry is available.

McKinley Village Lodge (Mile 231 Parks Hwy., 907/276-7234 or 800/276-7234, www. denaliparkresorts.com, $293-373 d) is along the Nenana River. Here you'll find 150 comfortable—and overpriced—hotel rooms, a café,

and lounge. It's run by Denali Park Resorts (Aramark), the park concessionaire.

Kantishna Lodges

This private inholding is deep within Denali, 92 miles out the Park Road. Originally a gold mining settlement, it now has several lodges and an air taxi operator. These upscale lodges are definitely not for budget travelers, and it's a long bus ride to Kantishna, so most guests stay at least three nights in this very scenic area. All five of the lodges are open only early June-mid-September. Private buses transport visitors to the lodges at Kantishna, or you can fly out on Kantishna Air Taxi (907/644-8222, www. katair.com). There is no cell phone service in the Kantishna area.

At **Kantishna Roadhouse** (907/683-8003 summer or 800/942-7420, www.kantishn-aroadhouse.com, June-mid-Sept., $910 d per day) the all-inclusive rate includes lodging in cabins or duplex rooms, meals, bus

Denali Mountain Morning Hostel and Lodge

© DON PITCHER

transportation from the park entrance, dogsled demonstrations, mountain bikes, gold panning, guided hikes, and interpretive programs. A bar and restaurant are on the premises. A two-night minimum stay is required.

Two wonderful Kantishna lodges—Camp Denali and North Face Lodge—have the same management and contacts. At both places, the emphasis is on the natural world, with guided hikes, mountain biking, canoeing, fishing, evening programs, and delicious meals, and the rates are all-inclusive. Established in 1952, **C Camp Denali** (907/683-2290, www.campdenali.com, early June-mid-Sept., three nights: $1,635 adults, $1,226 children under 12; four nights: $2,180 adults, $1,635 children under) has spectacular views of Mount McKinley, and is operated as a low-key wilderness retreat for a maximum of 40 guests. International experts lead special programs throughout the summer, focusing on such topics as bird conservation, nature photography, mountaineering, photography, northern lights, and environmental issues. Lodging is in 18 cozy cabins with woodstoves, propane

lights, an outhouse, and a shower building. If you can't handle an outhouse, book a room at North Face Lodge instead.

One mile from Camp Denali is **C North Face Lodge** (907/683-2290, www.campdenali.com, early June-mid-Sept., three nights: $1,635 adults, $1,226 children under 12; four nights: $2,180 adults, $1,635 children under), which is operated more like a country inn, with 15 guest rooms, all containing private baths. The all-inclusive price includes lodging, food, bus transportation to and from Kantishna, lectures, guided hikes, and other activities. Guests must stay at least three nights, with fixed arrival and departure dates.

Denali Backcountry Lodge (907/644-9980 or 877/233-6254, www.denalilodge.com, early June-mid-Sept., $930-1,070 d per day) has cabins and a main lodge at the end of the road. The cabins—all with private baths and one or two beds—range from basic units with no view to nicer ones with decks along the creek. The all-inclusive rates are for two people per day. Rates includes round-trip transport by bus into the park, meals, bikes, fishing, and naturalist presentations. There are no TVs, Wi-Fi, or cell phone coverage. It's a long ride, so some guests opt to ride the bus in and fly back out on Kantishna Air (an extra $150 pp).

Operated by the owners of Kantishna Air Taxi, **Skyline Lodge** (Mile 92 Park Rd., 907/644-8222, www.katair.com, June-Sept., $265 d, $384 for two people including lodging and meals) provides the least expensive accommodations in Kantishna. The solar-powered lodge can accommodate up to 10 guests in four cabins, each with a queen bed downstairs plus a sleeping loft with double bed. The bathroom and showers are in the main lodge, and phone and Internet are very limited.

Park Campgrounds

Inside Denali National Park are six campgrounds, four of which have evening nature programs throughout the summer. Riley Creek, Savage River, Teklanika River, and Wonder Lake campgrounds can be reserved in advance through **Doyan/Aramark** (907/272-7275 or 800/622-7275, www.reservedenali. com, $5 reservation fee) starting in mid-February. You can also reserve campsites at the visitor centers if they aren't already full, but this is definitely *not* a wise move if you want any choice of where you stay.

You can drive to Riley Creek, Savage River, and Teklanika River campgrounds, so they fill up fast. Otherwise, campground access is via the **camper buses** (adults $33, kids free).

RILEY CREEK CAMPGROUND

Largest and most accessible campground in the park, Riley Creek Campground ($22-28 pull-in sites, $14 walk-in sites, free in winter) has 146 sites just a quarter-mile off the Parks Highway. It's open year-round, with bear-proof food lockers, running water, and flush toilets, but limited facilities and no water September-May. This campground is very popular with RVers and car campers, but suffers somewhat from highway

noise. Park rangers provide evening nature programs, and the adjacent **Riley Creek Mercantile** provides firewood, a few supplies, a dump station, coin laundry, $5 showers, and free Wi-Fi.

SAVAGE RIVER CAMPGROUND

Near the end of the paved, publicly accessible portion of the Park Road, Savage River Campground (Mile 13 Park Rd., late May-mid-Sept., $22, $28 pull-through sites, $40 group sites) has 33 wooded sites for vehicles and tents, with bear-proof lockers and flush and vault toilets. Two group sites (tents only) are available. You'll need to bring firewood for campfires.

SANCTUARY RIVER CAMPGROUND

Remote and tranquil, Sanctuary River Campground (Mile 23 Park Rd., late May-mid-Sept., $9) contains seven heavily forested tent sites. The campground has vault toilets and bear-proof lockers, but no potable water. You'll need to bring water or filter it from the silty river, and campfires aren't allowed. Unlike most Denali campgrounds, reservations aren't taken for Sanctuary River; check at the Wilderness Access Center or Riley Creek Mercantile to see if sites are available. No vehicles are allowed here, so access is only via the camper bus.

TEKLANIKA RIVER CAMPGROUND

Teklanika River Campground (Mile 29 Park Rd., late May-mid-Sept., $16) provides 53 forested sites for tents and vehicles. The braided Teklanika River provides an easy gravel surface for day hikes from the campground, and this is the farthest point RVs can drive into the park. Vault toilets and running water are provided, along with bear-proof food storage, but bring firewood with you (available at Riley Creek Mercantile) if you want a campfire, since none is available for sale.

There's a three-night minimum stay for vehicular campers at Tek, and your vehicle must stay at your campsite for the duration of your stay. It can only leave when you're driving back out of the park. There is no minimum stay requirement for campers arriving on the camper bus since they don't have a private vehicle.

Campers at Teklanika should purchase a **"Tek Pass"** for each member of your party. This allows you to use the park shuttle buses throughout your stay at Teklanika Campground for the price of just one trip; it's only available for travel farther into the park, not back to the park entrance.

IGLOO CREEK CAMPGROUND

Hemmed in by the mountains, little Igloo Creek Campground (Mile 35 Park Rd., late May-mid-Sept., $9) features seven wooded tent-only sites. The campground has pit vault toilets, but you'll need to bring plenty of water or a filter. Fires are not permitted and vehicles aren't allowed, so you'll need to arrive via the camper bus. Reservations aren't taken for Igloo Creek Campground, so stop by the Wilderness Access Center or Riley Creek Mercantile to see if sites are available. There's great hiking around Igloo Creek, with relatively easy access to the high country.

WONDER LAKE CAMPGROUND

Wonder Lake Campground (Mile 85 Park Rd., early June-mid-Sept., $16) has 28 tent-only sites in one of the most dramatic settings anywhere on the planet. The country is rolling tundra, with a few trees and the potential to see Mount McKinley in all its glory (if the weather cooperates). The lake—2.7 miles long by 0.5 miles wide—is a short walk away. Wonder Lake Campground has running water, flush toilets, cooking shelters, and bear storage lockers. Because of its location, Wonder Lake doesn't open until early June. Make reservations well ahead for campsites here, especially when fall colors peak in late August and early September.

RV Parks

Denali Rainbow Village (907/683-7777, www.

denalirv.com, mid-May-mid-Sept., RVs $38-42, tents $25) is in the heart of the Denali Park/Glitter Gulch action, with a big lot behind the row of buildings on the east side of the road. It has a laundry, Wi-Fi, and cable TV. Showers are $5 if you aren't camping here.

Eight miles south of the park entrance is **Denali Grizzly Bear Resort** (907/683-2696 or 866/583-2696, www.denaligrizzlybear.com, RVs $38, tents $25, tent cabins $38). Showers, laundry, a central cooking shelter, and Wi-Fi (fee) are available.

Fourteen miles south of the park is **Denali Mountain Morning Hostel and Lodge** (907/683-7503, www.denalihostel.com, early May-late Sept., wall tents $32 s, $55 d). There is no camping, but it does have creekside wall tents, with sleeping bags, cots, a bathhouse, central kitchen, computer, laundry, free Wi-Fi, and free park shuttle. Additional RV parks are in Healy, 11 miles north of the park entrance.

FOOD

A number of places offer pricey summertime eats just north of the park entrance at the packed settlement of businesses called The Canyon, Denali Park, Denali, or Glitter Gulch; most are shuttered when the tourists flee south after mid-September.

Cafés and Diners

Begin your day at **Black Bear Coffee House** (Mile 238 Parks Hwy., 907/683-1656, daily 6:30am-10pm mid-May-mid-Sept., $5-10) with eggy breakfasts, bagels, espresso, sandwiches, and muffins, plus "$5 after 5" deal with burritos and grilled cheese in the evening. The café also has Wi-Fi, a free guest computer, and a loaner iPad ($3 for 30 minutes), along with occasional live music on the deck. Expect a long wait most mornings.

If you're just hankering for that old standby, head over to **Great Alaska Fish & Chips Co.** (Mile 238.9 Parks Hwy., 907/683-3474, www.

alaskafishandchip.com, daily 10:30am-9pm mid-May-mid-Sept., $15-17) for a big serving of halibut or cod fish and chips. There's a salad bar and a handful of other choices too, including burgers, sandwiches, and cold pitchers of Alaskan Amber.

One of the better restaurants in the Denali area is 11 miles south of the park entrance: **McKinley Creekside Café** (Mile 224 Parks Hwy., 907/683-2277 or 888/533-6254, www. mckinleycabins.com, daily 6am-10pm mid-May-mid-Sept., $15-23). You'll find good breakfasts (including gigantic half-pound cinnamon rolls), homemade soups, sandwiches, and gyros for lunch, plus meatloaf, pasta specials, and fresh chicken pot pie in the evening, along with Friday night prime rib and filling box lunches ($13). The little deck is perfect for mid-summer dining. Pop open your laptop for free Wi-Fi.

Bar and Grills

In business for more than 25 years, **Denali Salmon Bake** (Mile 238.5 Parks Hwy., 907/683-2733, www.denaliparksalmonbake. com, daily 7am-11pm mid-May-late Sept., $20-29) is extremely popular and quite reasonable for breakfast, lunch, and dinner. When you step into this rustic old building the slanting floors are immediate evidence of the melting permafrost beneath the structure; the slope increases by an inch or two each year! The Bake's diverse menu stars apple stuffed waffles and stampede scramble skillet for breakfast, sourdough grilled cheese sandwiches and Alaska buffalo burgers for lunch, plus baby back ribs, halibut and chips, or king salmon for dinner. The restaurant has Wi-Fi and a **free shuttle** to local hotels, campgrounds, and the Wilderness Access Center. A sprawling upstairs no-smoking bar comes alive with bluegrass and folk bands four nights a week, and has 21 beers on tap, along with an enormous frozen blue concoction called the McKinley margarita. Join all the Bulgarian, Serbian, and Slavic seasonal workers for Wednesday-night "J-1" dance parties. Heading into the park? Have the "Bake" make a big box lunch ($13). Hungry late? Halibut tacos are available till the bar closes at 4am. The Salmon Bake's owners seem to have half the local businesses, with seven different places at last count, including Prospectors Pizza, 49th State Brewing Co., and Miners Market & Deli.

Pizza

On the north end of the Glitter Gulch action, **Prospectors Pizzeria & Alehouse** (Mile 238.9 Parks Hwy., 907/683-7437, www.prospectorspizza.com, daily 11am-10 or later mid-May-late Sept., pizzas $20-29 for a 17-incher) gets packed with folks most summer evenings, so be ready for a 45-minute wait. In addition to wood stone brick oven pizzas, the menu includes salads, pastas, sandwiches, and a locally famous baked tomato soup. There's outside seating and 49 beers on tap.

Right across the creek is **Panorama Pizza Pub** (Mile 224 Parks Hwy., 907/683-2623, www.panoramapizzapub.com, food daily until 11pm mid-May-mid-Sept., $21-32), with excellent pizzas and live bluegrass music Wednesday-Saturday nights. The Denali pizza is topped with pepperoni, sausage, olives, mushrooms, and green peppers. Slices only are available after 11pm, and the bar stays open till 3am. The pub provides a free shuttle from Denali Park.

Steak and Seafood

High atop the bluff behind Denali Park, **Alpenglow Restaurant** (Grande Denali Lodge, Mile 238 Parks Hwy., 907/683-8500 or 866/683-8500, www.denalialaska.com, daily 5am-10pm mid-May-mid-Sept., breakfast buffet $12-16, $19-31) has the most extraordinary vistas in the area. Wraparound windows face Denali National Park, and the high ceilings are accented by a beautiful timber-frame design. In addition to a good steak and seafood selection, there's a lighter bar menu with burgers, salads, and BBQ sliders. Call to reserve a window table for dinner. Breakfast buffets are a good stuff-yourself deal.

At ◖ **229 Parks Restaurant** (Mile 229 Parks Hwy., 907/683-2567, www.229parks. com, Fri.-Sat. 9am-9pm and Sun. 9am-1pm Jan.-late Apr., Tues.-Sun. 5pm-10pm late May-Sept., closed late Apr.-late May and Oct.-Dec., $24-36) the name is also the location: Mile 229 on the Parks Highway. Housed within a bright timber-frame building nine miles south of Denali Park, the restaurant serves a bistro-style menu that changes frequently. Organic locally-grown vegetables and free-range meats are used whenever possible. Dinner entrées include steak au poivre and wild Alaskan scallops. "Tavern fare" options ($10-16) such as Caesar salads, Parmesan aioli flatbreads, or bison burgers offer a less expensive option. Save room for their ice cream sandwich with homemade ice cream between dark chocolate cookies. In addition to dinner, the restaurant serves pastries and espresso for brunch. Don't come here in a hurry; service can be slow since everything is made fresh. Reservations are highly recommended since the restaurant fills most nights; call several days ahead. The restaurant doesn't provide a shuttle, so you'll need your own wheels or a taxi ride from Denali Park.

Sweets

Denali Glacier Scoops (Mile 238 Parks Hwy., 907/683-6002, daily 11am-10pm mid-May-mid-Sept.) offers a double scoop of ice cream at Alaskan prices ($6). Also available are shakes, sundaes, soft serve, and smoothies.

Markets

Canyon Market and Cafe (Mile 238.4 Parks Hwy., 907/683-7467, www.canyonmarketcafe. com, daily 6am-1:30am) makes deli sandwiches and pastries, and offers a decent selection of groceries and produce. There is free Wi-Fi here, too.

In the heart of the action, **Lynx Creek Store/The Park Mart** (Mile 238.6 Parks Hwy., 907/683-2548, 8am-10pm summer) is a quickie-mart with some of the most expensive gas on the road system, along with such essentials as soda, sweets, and limited food items. The store also rents mountain and hybrid bikes ($20 for a half-day, $30 for all day).

INFORMATION AND SERVICES

The large Denali Park hotels all have **ATMs,** as does the Lynx Creek Store (Mile 238.6 Parks Hwy., 907/683-2548, 8am-10pm summer). A **post office** is adjacent to the Riley Creek Campground inside the park.

For medical help, head to **Canyon Clinic at Denali** (Parks Hwy., close to Denali Princess Lodge, 907/683-4433, daily in the summer). The nearest hospital is in Fairbanks.

GETTING THERE

The **Alaska Railroad's** *Denali Star* (907/265-2494 or 800/544-0552, www.alaskarailroad. com) leaves Fairbanks at 8:15am and arrives at Denali at noon ($51 one way); it departs Anchorage at 8:15am, arriving at Denali at 3:45pm ($117 one way).

Several companies have van transportation to Denali from Anchorage, Talkeetna, or Fairbanks. **Alaska/Yukon Trails** (907/479-2277 or 888/770-7275, www.alaskashuttle. com, daily Apr.-Sept.) connects Denali with Anchorage ($75 pp one-way), Talkeetna ($65 pp one-way), and Fairbanks ($55 pp one-way).

The **Alaska Bus Guy** (907/720-6541, www. alaskabusguy.com, daily in summer, twice-weekly in winter, $67 one way) operates an environmentally friendly hydrogen-hybrid van with runs between Anchorage (or Talkeetna) and Denali.

Park Connection (907/245-0200 or 800/266-8625, www.alaskacoach.com, mid-May-mid-Sept.) provides daily service connecting Denali with Talkeetna ($65), Anchorage ($80-90), Whittier ($155), and Seward ($155).

Local air taxis include **Denali Air** (Mile 229 Parks Hwy., 907/683-2261, www.denaliair.com), which operates from eight miles south of the park entrance, **Fly Denali** (a.k.a. Talkeetna Aero Services, 907/683-2899 or 888/733-2899, www.talkeetnaaero.com) from Healy, and **Kantishna Air Taxi** (907/644-8222, www.ka-tair.com) from Kantishna deep inside the park. **Era Helicopters** (907/683-2574 or 800/843-1947, www.eraflightseeing.com) is based next to the river in Denali Park.

GETTING AROUND

Call **Denali Transportation** (907/683-4765, www.denalitaxishuttle.com) for taxi service in the Healy/Denali Park area.

The Park Service's **Riley Creek Loop Bus** (5am-7pm mid-May-mid-Sept., free) provides service connecting the Riley Creek Campground, Wilderness Access Center, and train depot every half hour. In addition, a second free bus connects the Wilderness Access Center with the dogsled demonstrations at park headquarters, and the free Savage River Shuttle continues to Savage River Bridge at Mile 15.

Private shuttle buses are provided by local hotels. **Denali Salmon Bake** (Mile 238.5 Parks Hwy., 907/683-2733, www.denaliparksalmonbake.com, $1-2 one-way) provides a 24-hour shuttle that stops at the Wilderness Access Center, train depot, Denali Park/Canyon hotels and restaurants, and Healy businesses. The shuttle also stops at Riley Creek Campground upon request (call for a campground pickup).

HEALY AND VICINITY

Located 11 miles north of the turnoff to Denali National Park at Mile 249 of the Parks Highway, the town of Healy (pop. 640) has most of the necessities of life, including gas stations (considerably cheaper than at Denali Park), convenience stores, restaurants, a coin laundry, and a medical clinic.

Healy has grown up around the coal mining

that has operated here since the 1930s. **Usibelli Coal Mine** (907/683-2226, www.usibelli.com) is the largest in Alaska, which isn't saying much, since it's Alaska's *only* commercial coal mine. However, its 1.5 million tons of subbituminous coal mined each year does say something: a 4-million-pound "walking dragline" digs 1,000 cubic yards of overburden every hour, exposing the seams. The coal is shipped to Korea or used at an adjacent power plant that supplies the Tanana Valley and Fairbanks. Coal burning is a big factor in the earth's rapid warming. There's a certain irony in Alaska as the source of the coal that is leading to drastic changes across the state. Healy also benefits greatly from tourism to nearby Denali National Park.

Two miles south of town, play a round of golf at the nine-hole **Black Diamond Golf Course** (Otto Lake Rd., 907/683-4653, www.blackdiamondgolf.com, wagon ride: $89 adults, $39 kids) or take a three-hour covered wagon ride.

Accommodations

Add a seven percent tax to all Healy lodging rates.

[C] **Earth Song Lodge** (Stampede Rd., 907/683-2863, www.earthsonglodge.com, year-round, small cabins $155 d, family-size cabins $185 d, two-bedroom cabins $215 d, add $10 pp for extra adult guests) rents 12 cozy cabins, all with private baths. The cabins are all very clean and well-maintained. Earth Song is four miles down Stampede Road off the Parks Highway at Mile 251. Earth Song is open all year, with a nightly slide show at the coffeehouse, Wi-Fi in the lodge, and guided winter dogsledding into Denali National Park. Co-owner Jon Nierenberg is a former Denali park ranger and his wife Karin is an accomplished author.

Three miles south of Healy is **Denali RV Park and Motel** (Mile 245.1 Parks Hwy., 907/683-1500 or 800/478-1501, www.denalirvpark.com, late May-early Sept., $79 d, family units $139), with tiny motel rooms with private baths and family units with kitchens for four people. Units have cable TV, and there is Wi-Fi in the office.

White Moose Lodge (Mile 248 Parks Hwy., 907/683-1231 or 800/481-1232, www.white-mooselodge.com, early May-late Sept., $105 d) has 15 reasonably priced no-frills motel rooms with two double beds, satellite TVs, breakfast pastries and juice, and Wi-Fi.

Denali Park Hotel (Mile 247 Parks Hwy., 907/683-1800 or 866/683-1800, www.den-aliparkhotel.com, $119-139 d, add $10 pp for extra guests) is something of a misnomer. This 12-room motel has parking right outside your door and spacious older rooms with queen or king beds, fridges, microwaves, satellite TVs, and Wi-Fi. The motel lobby is a World War II-era Alaska Railroad railcar, and a complimentary shuttle is provided for visitors arriving by train.

Park's Edge Log Cabin Accommodations (Hilltop Ln., 907/683-4343, www.parks-edge.com, late May-early Sept., cabins $100-125 d, add $10 pp for extra guests, maximum of six) has modern economical cabins and a larger cabin. The cabins are adjacent to Black Diamond Golf Course. All include private baths and Wi-Fi.

Open all year, **Motel Nord Haven** (Mile 249 Parks Hwy., 907/683-4500 or 800/683-4501, www.motelnordhaven.com, year-round, $152 one queen bed, $170 two queen beds, $180 kitchenette unit) has nicely appointed rooms, hot breakfasts, a guest computer, and Wi-Fi. Request a room in the quieter annex building if possible. Rose's Café is next door.

It's hard to miss the geodesic-shaped **Denali Dome Home B&B** (Healy Spur Rd., 907/683-1239 or 800/683-1239, www.denalidomehome.com, year-round, $180 d), where lodging is available in a unique 7,000-square-foot house with rock fireplaces and seven guest rooms, all with king or queen beds, flat screen TV, and private baths. Two rooms contain jetted tubs, and guests appreciate the sauna, seven acres of parklike grounds and flower gardens, Wi-Fi, extensive art collection, and traditional cook-to-order breakfasts.

Touch of Wilderness B&B (2.9 Stampede Rd., 907/683-2459 or 800/683-2459, www.touchofwildernessbb.com, year-round, $165-198 d) is a 7,000-square-foot home in a quiet location 5 miles north of Healy along Stampede Road and 16 miles north of the park entrance. The nine guest rooms—one handicap accessible—have a variety of configurations and beds, plus private baths, self-serve breakfasts, comfortable common areas with fireplaces and TVs, and Wi-Fi.

Denali Lakeview Inn (Otto Lake Rd., 907/683-4035, www.denalilakeviewinn.com, $139-209 d) is a large place right on Otto Lake with 20 bright guest rooms and suites, plus in-room continental breakfast and Wi-Fi. The main attraction here is the spectacular lake-and-mountains view from the deck.

An immaculate modern home in a quiet neighborhood, **C Denali Primrose B&B** (1 Stoney Creek Dr., Healy, 907/683-1234, www.denaliprimrose.com, one-bedroom suite $126 d, three-bedroom suite $172 d, add $15 pp for extra guests) has two suites. Lodging options are a downstairs one-bedroom suite and a three-bedroom upstairs suite with a whirlpool tub. Amenities include private baths, TVs, Wi-Fi, continental breakfasts, and a gracious owner.

Aspen Haus B&B (907/683-2004, www.aspenhaus.com, late May-early Sept., cabins $129-179 d, suites $145 d) has a quiet in-the-trees setting and four spacious cabins, the largest with room for six people, plus two upstairs suites. Each unit includes private baths, queen beds, a fridge, a microwave, Wi-Fi, and breakfast ingredients.

Operated by the Denali Outdoor Center, **Otto Lake Cabins & Camping** (Otto Lake Rd., 907/683-1925 or 888/303-1925, www.

INTO THE WILD PHOTO-OP

© DON PITCHER

bus from the film *Into the Wild* in front of 49th State Brewery

A few miles north of Healy is the turnoff for the Stampede Road, made infamous in the book and movie *Into the Wild*. Access to the old bus where Chris McCandless died is very difficult. Here's what the locals tell folks trying to get there: "This is where you turn off the highway; this is where you park the car; this is where you get eaten to death by mosquitoes; this is where you might drown; this is where the bear mauls you; and this is where you starve to death and die." At least one person has died attempting to reach the bus, so don't take the chance. An identical replica of the Magic Bus–it was used in the movie–sits out front of 49th State Brewery in Healy. Take your photo there instead of risking your life!

denalioutdoorcenter.com, $92 d, $112 for four people) has economy cabins on the shore of this lake just two miles south of Healy. The cabins share a shower house, laundry, and kitchen facility.

Camping

Three miles south of Healy, **Denali RV Park and Motel** (Mile 245.1 Parks Hwy., 907/683-1500 or 800/478-1501, www.denalirvpark.com, late May-early Sept., RVs $40, showers $3) has nicely maintained RV spaces and clean showers. There is free Wi-Fi and cable TV.

McKinley RV and Campground (Mile 248.5 Parks Hwy., 907/683-1418 or 800/478-2562, www.mckinleyrv.com, May-Sept., RVs $38, tents $15) occupies a somewhat wooded area just off the highway. The campground gets complaints about cleanliness and maintenance, so you may want to check it out first, but there's free Wi-Fi and a shuttle to the park. It's adjacent to 49th State Brewing Co. and the Chevron gas station with its 24-hour convenience store, deli, ATM, espresso, laundry, and liquor store.

Two miles south of Healy, **Otto Lake Cabins & Camping** (Otto Lake Rd., 907/683-1925 or 888/303-1925, www.denalioutdoor-center.com, mid-May-mid-Sept., $8 pp) has lakeside campsites. Potable water is provided and outhouses are available, along with showers ($5), a laundry ($5), and canoe and bike rentals ($8/hour).

Food

Healy's main attraction is **49th State Brewery** (Mile 248.5 Parks Hwy., 907/683-2739, www.49statebrewing.com, daily noon-1:30am mid-Mar.-Oct., $16-33), a cavernous industrial-style building with a pub menu of burgers, sandwiches, pizzas, and munchies served all day, plus such dinner entrées as alderwood smoked ribs, beer battered shrimp tacos, and Alaskan ribeye steak. There's a pig roast every Thursday, and all-you-can-eat pork on Fridays. The brewery produces seven or so beers, including the popular Baked Blonde Ale, and also has a good choice of cocktails, wine, and more than 130 whiskeys. Food is served till 1:30am, with a limited menu after 11pm. The pub provides a free shuttle van to Denali Park, and has live music on the patio most summer weekends. Parked out front is the bus used in the *Into the Wild* movie; it's a replica of the real one a few miles away.

Find a lounge and a 24-hour restaurant with family fare and pizzas at **Totem Inn** (Mile 249 Parks Hwy., 907/683-6500, www.thetoteminn.com, daily 7am-10pm).

Try the bacon cheeseburgers and other home-cooked food at friendly **Rose's Café** (Mile 249.5 Parks Hwy., 907/683-7673, www.rosescafealaska.com, daily 6:30am-9:30pm Mar.-late Oct., $11-16), open for three meals a day. There's a "Grizzly Wall of Fame" for anyone who eats Rose's infamous one-pound grizzly burger (topped with an egg and a slice of ham) plus the side order of fires and potato salad. **Henry's Coffeehouse at Earth Song Lodge** (Stampede Rd., 907/683-2863, www.earthsonglodge.com, breakfast and dinner in summer) serves bagels, baked goods, soups, sandwiches, salads, pizzas, and espresso.

The **Black Diamond Grill** (Otto Lake Rd., 907/683-4653, www.blackdiamondgolf.com, daily 11am-11pm, $18-36) serves a menu of prime rib sandwiches, steaks, and halibut. The restaurant has a free shuttle bus if you're staying in Healy or Denali Park hotels. It's owned by the Usibelli family, which also operates the coal mine in Healy and Usibelli Vineyards in Napa Valley.

Information and Services

There is no local visitor center, but the **Denali Chamber of Commerce** (907/683-4636, www.denalichamber.com) will send you local brochures. For medical care, head to **Interior Community Health Center** (Usibelli Spur Rd., 907/683-2211, www.myhealthclinic.org); a physician's assistant and nurse are on call.

Getting There and Around

Denali Salmon Bake shuttle (Mile 238.5 Parks Hwy., 907/683-2733, www.denaliparksalmonbake.com, $1 one way, $2 to Wilderness Access Center) provides a 24-hour summertime shuttle that operates every 1.5 hours, stopping at the Wilderness Access Center, train depot, Denali Park/Canyon hotels and restaurants, 49th State Brewing, Miners Market, and McKinley RV in Healy. The shuttle also stops at Riley Creek Campground upon request (call for a campground pickup).

Call **Denali Transportation** (907/683-4765, www.denalitaxishuttle.com) for taxi service in the Healy/Denali Park area.

The owners of Denali Dome Home B&B provide rental cars through **Keys to Denali** (907/683-5397 or 800/683-1239, www.denalidomehome.com, $110-150/day), and provide pick ups and drop offs anywhere in the area, including the Denali train station. This is a great way to explore the area without having to drive all the way from Anchorage.

www.moon.com

DESTINATIONS | ACTIVITIES | BLOGS | MAPS | BOOKS

MOON.COM is ready to help plan your next trip! Filled with fresh trip ideas and strategies, author interviews, informative travel blogs, a detailed map library, and descriptions of all the Moon guidebooks, Moon.com is all you need to get out and explore the world—or even places in your own backyard. While at Moon.com, sign up for our monthly e-newsletter for updates on new releases, travel tips, and expert advice from our on-the-go Moon authors. As always, when you travel with Moon, expect an experience that is uncommon and truly unique.

KEEP UP WITH MOON ON FACEBOOK AND TWITTER
JOIN THE MOON PHOTO GROUP ON FLICKR

MAP SYMBOLS

≈≈≈ Expressway	〔 Highlight	✗ Airfield	↓ Golf Course	
Primary Road	○ City/Town	✗ Airport	🅿 Parking Area	
Secondary Road	◉ State Capital	▲ Mountain	🔺 Archaeological Site	
Unpaved Road	⊛ National Capital	✛ Unique Natural Feature	⬆ Church	
Trail	★ Point of Interest			
Ferry	• Accommodation	⬘ Waterfall	🅂 Gas Station	
Railroad	▼ Restaurant/Bar	▲ Park	Glacier	
Pedestrian Walkway	■ Other Location	◻ Trailhead	Mangrove	
Stairs	△ Campground	✘ Skiing Area	Reef	
			Swamp	

CONVERSION TABLES

°C = (°F - 32) / 1.8
°F = (°C x 1.8) + 32
1 inch = 2.54 centimeters (cm)
1 foot = 0.304 meters (m)
1 yard = 0.914 meters
1 mile = 1.6093 kilometers (km)
1 km = 0.6214 miles
1 fathom = 1.8288 m
1 chain = 20.1168 m
1 furlong = 201.168 m
1 acre = 0.4047 hectares
1 sq km = 100 hectares
1 sq mile = 2.59 square km
1 ounce = 28.35 grams
1 pound = 0.4536 kilograms
1 short ton = 0.90718 metric ton
1 short ton = 2,000 pounds
1 long ton = 1.016 metric tons
1 long ton = 2,240 pounds
1 metric ton = 1,000 kilograms
1 quart = 0.94635 liters
1 US gallon = 3.7854 liters
1 Imperial gallon = 4.5459 liters
1 nautical mile = 1.852 km

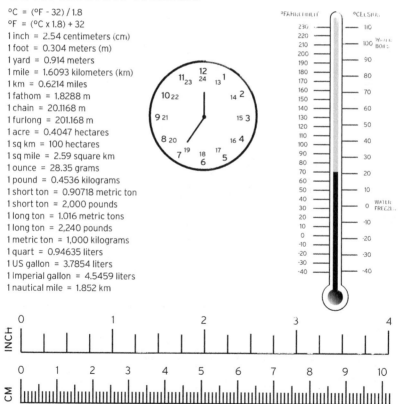

MOON SPOTLIGHT DENALI NATIONAL PARK

Avalon Travel
a member of the Perseus Books Group
1700 Fourth Street
Berkeley, CA 94710, USA
www.moon.com

Editor: Leah Gordon
Series Manager: Kathryn Ettinger
Copy Editor: Naomi Adler Dancis
Graphics Coordinator: Kathryn Osgood
Production Coordinator: Elizabeth Jang
Cover Designer: Darren Alessi
Map Editor: Mike Morgenfeld
Cartographer: Chris Henrick

ISBN-13: 978-1-61238-984-4

Front cover photo: large broomed dall sheep ram in Denali National Park © twildlife/istockphoto.com

Title Page photo: The famous green bus that transports visitors into and out of Denali National Park © David Barnard/123rf.com

Printed in the United States of America

All recommendations, including those for sights, activities, hotels, restaurants, and shops, are based on each author's individual judgment. We do not accept payment for inclusion in our travel guides, and our authors don't accept free goods or services in exchange for positive coverage.

Although every effort was made to ensure that the information was correct at the time of going to press, the author and publisher do not assume and hereby disclaim any liability to any party for any loss or damage caused by errors, omissions, or any potential travel disruption due to labor or financial difficulty, whether such errors or omissions result from negligence, accident, or any other cause.

ABOUT THE AUTHOR

Don Pitcher

Perhaps Don Pitcher's love of travel came about because he moved so much as a child; by age 15 he had lived in six states and two dozen East Coast and Midwestern towns. Don's family hails from Maine, but he was born in Atlanta, making him a southerner with New England blood. He moved west for college, receiving a master's degree from the University of California, Berkeley, where his thesis examined wildfires in the high elevation forests of Sequoia National Park. When his first (and only) scientific paper was published, he appeared to be headed into the world of ecological research.

Don then landed what seemed like the coolest job on the planet shortly after grad school: being flown around Alaska's massive Wrangell-St. Elias National Park in a helicopter while conducting fire research. Wild places continued to beckon, and over the next 15 years Don built backcountry trails, worked as a wilderness ranger, mapped grizzly bear habitats, and operated salmon weirs – anything to avoid an office job. After that first season in Alaska, he spent three months in the South Pacific, and quickly found himself addicted to travel. His explorations eventually took him to 35 countries and all 50 states.

After authoring his first book, *Berkeley Inside/Out*, Don went on to write *Moon Yellowstone & Grand Teton*, *Moon Alaska*, *Moon Wyoming*, *Moon San Juan Islands*, and *Moon Anchorage, Denali & the Kenai Peninsula*. He has produced three photographic books, served as editor for *Best Places Alaska*, and is a contributor to Triporati.com and other websites. Don's photos have appeared in a multitude of publications and advertisements, and his prints are sold in many Alaska and Washington galleries. He is also a highly regarded wedding photographer.

Don lives in Homer, Alaska, with his wife, Karen Shemet, and their children, Aziza and Rio. Get details on his latest writing and photography projects – along with links to many of the places mentioned in this book – at www.DonPitcher.com, or find him on Facebook.

CPSIA information can be obtained at www.ICGtesting.com
Printed in the USA
LVOW04s2018201114

414775LV00001B/1/P